THE TEN(DER) COMMANDMENTS

THE TEN(DER) COMMANDMENTS

Reflections on the Father's Love

RON MEHL

Multnomah Publishers *Sisters, Oregon*

THE TEN(DER) COMMANDMENTS
Published by Multnomah Publishers, Inc.
© 1998 by Ron Mehl

International Standard Book Number: 1-57673-304-1

Cover design by D² Designworks
Cover photograph by Uniphoto

Printed in the United States of America

Most Scripture quotations are from: *The Holy Bible, The New King James Version*
© 1984 by Thomas Nelson, Inc.

also quoted:
The Holy Bible, New International Version (NIV) © 1973, 1984 by International Bible
Society, used by permission of Zondervan Publishing House.

New American Standard Bible (NASB)
© 1960, 1977 by the Lockman Foundation

The New Testament in Modern English (Phillips) © 1958 by J. B. Phillips

The Living Bible (TLB) © 1971. Used by permission of Tyndale House Publishers, Inc.
All rights reserved.

Holy Bible, New Living Translation (NLT) © 1996. Used by permission of Tyndale House
Publishers, Inc. All rights reserved.

The Modern Language Bible, New Berkeley Version (MLB) © 1945, 1959, 1969 by
Zondervan Publishing House

The Amplified Bible (AMP) © 1965, 1987 by Zondervan Publishing House

Multnomah is a registered trademark of Multnomah Publishers, Inc. The colophon is
a trademark of Multnomah Publishers, Inc.

For information:
Multnomah Publishers, Inc.•Post Office Box 1720•Sisters, Oregon 97759

Library of Congress Cataloging-in-Publication Data:
  The Ten(der) commandments: reflections on the Father's love/Ron Mehl.
    p.cm.   Includes bibliographical references.   ISBN 1-57673-304-1 (alk. paper)
  1. Ten commandments.   2. God—Love—Biblical teaching.   I. Title.
BV4655.M434   1998   98–23085   241.5'.2—dc21   CIP

98 99 00 01 02 03 04 05 — 10 9 8 7 6 5 4 3 2

I feel honored to dedicate this book to the men and women I have esteemed in the faith and hold in highest regard. Their lives have modeled for me God's tender commandments in so many ways. Some of them were missionaries and pastors, and some were my Sunday school teachers. Their passion for souls, uncommon lives, and commitment to communicating the gospel of Christ have profoundly shaped my life. They have shown me that daily strength comes from daily prayer, and that if you'll obey God's commands and do the possible, He will do the impossible. I feel privileged to honor these beloved saints of the cross.

CONTENTS

ACKNOWLEDGMENTS

You know the expression "How do I love thee? Let me count the ways." Elizabeth Barrett Browning wrote those words in the mid-1800s. Because of her ill health, she wanted to express to her husband how much she loved him. So she sat down and penned a list of reasons to make it plain and clear.

Now I find myself in a situation just like Elizabeth's. I want some people to know how much I love them for making this book possible. First let me say I could never count the ways. I owe an incredible debt of gratitude to a number of people who spoke into my life and gave me valuable help. To Rev. Dennis Easter, insightful in the Word and a dear friend. To my coworkers Rev. Rob Anthony, Rev. Keith Reetz, and Rev. Chuck Updike, who gave me helpful suggestions. It seems I drain their hearts for ideas every day. To April Westbrook, a professor of Pentateuch, who answered my toughest questions. And to Dr. Dick Scott, a lifelong friend who answers whenever I call.

I am also greatly indebted to Gayle Potter and Debbie Matheny, who read and reread every chapter, every verse, every line. They don't miss much. They can sniff out an error like bloodhounds.

I want to thank Larry Libby, who has stuck with me from my first book until now. His editorial touch is unparalleled, but it's his calling me a friend that means the most. I think I've given him reason to question God when He says He'll never give us more than we can bear. I certainly have given Larry opportunity to question that verse of Scripture.

I want to say thanks to Don and Brenda Jacobson and the entire family at Multnomah. I never cease to be amazed at the grace that rests on that team of people. I feel privileged to be their friend.

And finally, I want to thank Joyce, my wife, who has provided me with more tenderness and love than I can handle or deserve. She was a cheerleader in college and still takes the time to lead a cheer for me that keeps me going.

And Moses went up to God, and the LORD called to him
from the mountain, saying, "Thus you shall say
to the house of Jacob, and tell the children of Israel:
"You have seen what I did to the Egyptians,
and how I bore you on eagles' wings
and brought you to Myself."

EXODUS 19:3–4

———

❧

ON EAGLES' WINGS

G O D   S E T S   T H E   C O N T E X T

Joyce's love letters always started out a little slow.

I was young, in college, in love, and in a hurry. And I couldn't help but note how her correspondence always moved along in low gear for the first few pages. You know what I mean. Chatty stuff. How are you, what do you think of the weather, how are classes, how's the family, how's basketball practice, and all that. Over time I learned to speed-read through those "preliminaries," knowing that I could (and would) go back to read the whole thing over again a couple thousand times.

But I wanted to jump right into the good stuff.

I wanted to read the parts that said how wonderful and charming I was…and what a godly, dedicated young man I was, and how she couldn't live without me. She did say some very nice, sweet things in those letters…but somehow, it was never quite enough. I not only wanted to absorb everything on the surface, I wanted to dive even deeper into that perfumed prose. I kept trying so very hard to read *between* those lines of neat, feminine cursive. She said this, but she obviously intended that.

She signed it thus and so but she probably wanted to sign it with a little more zing. She must have meant a lot more than she wrote. This was probably only the tip of the iceberg. If she'd had more time and paper and ink and postage, she would surely have said a lot more.

I could spend hours analyzing her words and phrases, looking for elusive code words and guessing at imagined secret meanings. Looking back, I realize now that I would have enjoyed life a lot more if I'd just relaxed and treasured her letters for what they were—instead of trying to bend them into what I wanted them to be. I really didn't *need* to read between the lines—the love was right there in front of me.

Have you ever heard the Ten Commandments described as a love letter…a tender, heartfelt message from the very hand of God? Perhaps not. Yet I've become convinced it is one of the most powerful expressions of God's love in all of Scripture. And you don't need to read between the lines! It's all there. He doesn't leave anything out. These ten statements are all-encompassing, touching virtually every part of our lives. They are the parameters to live by—the truths He knows are going to provide blessing and strength, a future and a hope.

There are several books out today on both the secular and Christian bestseller lists that purport to reveal a "secret code" embedded in the text of the Hebrew scriptures. These books talk about how computer technology has revealed an intricate pattern within the ancient texts—a code that supposedly names contemporary political leaders and spells out future events.

That's all very interesting, but to tell you the truth, I don't need any secret code. I don't need to read between the lines. I don't need to count all the letters and spaces, multiply them by seven, and divide them by twenty-two. I don't need to borrow a supercomputer from the defense department and an analyst from MIT. All I need to know is what God is plainly saying to me on the pages of my Bible. And if I miss the *real* message of these Ten Commandments, I've missed a great deal.

In fact, I've missed the very heart of God.

Some people, of course, imagine it to be the exact opposite. They don't hear love in these statements at all. What do they hear? They hear the clank of chains and the rattle of padlocks. They hear God saying, "You mess with Me, you step out of bounds, and I'll fry you like a bug landing on a transformer."

All of this, of course, plays right into Satan's master plan— the one he's had from the beginning. (Why change if it still works?) "God is a prude. God is a killjoy. God is a harsh old grandfather with a long, gray beard and bushy eyebrows who doesn't want anyone to have any fun—ever."

No, it's not a very original line of reasoning. The enemy began it with Eve back at the dawn of creation when he said, "Has God *really* forbidden you this lovely fruit? Oh my. What a pity. What a shame. He knows that if you ever tasted from this tree, you'd be like a god. Nothing could hold you back. You think the Garden of Eden is nice now? You ain't seen nothin'. God wants to keep you from the tang and sweetness of life. True freedom means freedom from confining restrictions such as these."

Is he right? Are the Ten Commandments harsh and negative…narrow and legalistic…cold and confining? Could there be a brighter, warmer, more passionate side to this familiar portion of Scripture we may have missed through the years? Is it possible we've misunderstood the first few pages of God's love letter, the very words that set the Ten Commandments in context?

Did you know that there was prior conversation between the Lord and Moses before He gave him those tablets of stone? Did you know that God gave Moses specific instructions about what to say to the people BEFORE presenting the Ten Commandments? *It was God Himself who set the context.* It's all right here in the book of Exodus.

Of course, Satan would rather we never learned these prior instructions. Why? Because it suits his purpose to quote God's words out of context. It always has. If he can't persuade you to stay away from the Bible, he'll try to wrench God's words out of their rightful settings. *And the rightful setting of the Ten Commandments is the boundless, faithful, Father-love of the living God.* Can you hear His heart beating in these words?

> And Moses went up to God, and the LORD called to him from the mountain, saying, "Thus you shall say to the house of Jacob, and tell the children of Israel: 'You have seen what I did to the Egyptians, and how I bore you on eagles' wings and brought you to Myself. Now therefore, if you will indeed obey My voice and keep My covenant, then you shall be a special treasure to Me above all people; for all the earth is Mine. And you shall be to Me a kingdom of priests and a holy nation.' These are the words which you shall speak to the children of Israel." (Exodus 19:3–6)

The Lord was saying, "Moses, before you give the people these commands, before anything else, will you please remind them that I bore them on eagles' wings?"

Why in the world would the Lord say that? It's a very endearing term. But when did He do that? When did the Lord bear them on eagles' wings? The people who originally heard these words knew very well what the Lord was talking about, because the memory was still fresh in their minds. The Lord was saying something like this…

"Do you remember when you were trapped in Egypt, and there was no place for you to go, and you were in bondage and in trouble? Do you remember when you groaned in your captivity because of the oppression and terrible cruelty of your taskmasters? Do you remember looking at your precious children and realizing there was no hope or future at all for them beyond chains, a lash, and early death?

"I heard your cries. I saw your tears. And I came down to buy you back out of your slavery. Do you remember, My children?

"Do you remember standing on the shore with the Red Sea lapping at your feet and Pharaoh's troops massing at your back? Do you remember the despair you felt because you couldn't go forward or back and death was riding toward you like a storm out of the west?

"I made a way for you where there was no way. Do you remember, My people?

"Do you remember those days in the wilderness where there was nothing to drink and your throats were dry and your little ones cried for water?

"I opened up a spring for you…a stream of fresh, sweet water came gushing over the parched desert floor. Do you remember, Israel?

"Do you remember being hungry in that barren place, with no provisions and no supplies? I fed you every day with manna, the bread of angels. You faced foreign armies, enemies greater and stronger than you, but I fought for you. In the times you thought you would never make it, that you would never survive, that there was no way in the world you could endure, I was watching all the time. I stepped into your lives to save you.

"I swooped down and bore you on eagles' wings; do you remember?"

That is the context of the ten statements in Exodus 20:1–17. And that is something you may have never considered before.

Did the Lord deliver these people out of four hundred years of slavery in Egypt just to browbeat them and brutalize them in the wilderness? Do we ever stop to consider just how much the Lord longed after these people and delighted in them?

Centuries after those days in the Sinai, the Lord told the prophet Hosea:

"When I found Israel,
　　it was like finding grapes in the desert;
when I saw your fathers,
　　it was like seeing the early fruit on the fig tree."
(Hosea 9:10, NIV)

What are grapes in the desert and early fruit on the fig tree? They are refreshing delicacies. They are something to bring a surge of pure pleasure to the heart. And in His love, in the fullness of His delight for these people that He had redeemed, the Lord penned them one of the most profound love letters of all time…a reminder of His eternal love. He wrote it with His own hand, the very finger of God.

One of my fondest memories was getting up one morning when Joyce had left for a women's retreat and finding little yellow Post-it notes from her just about everywhere I looked. I found one on the bathroom mirror that said, "Have a nice day. I love you very much." There was another on the refrigerator door, another on the toaster, another on my briefcase, and another *in* my briefcase. There was one on the steering wheel of my car, on the chair in my office, and on my study table. It seemed that wherever I went that day I'd find a little yellow tab with a simple reminder of her love for me.

What a great feeling! I was surrounded by messages of this woman's love. They were low and high. They were on my left and on my right. They reached me coming in and going out.

Maybe Israel didn't see those little sticky notes from God, but the truth is, He posted them everywhere. They were on the sand where they knelt to drink from the cool stream God caused to bubble up right out of the arid desert. They were on the desert floor in the morning when they gathered the fresh manna, sweet as honey. They were on the empty helmets of the Egyptian soldiers, tossed up on the sand by the waves. Deliverance! Release! Protection! Provision!

"I bore you on eagles' wings."

What does that mean, anyway? If you were a regular reader of *Ranger Rick* magazine, you would know very well what that means. A mama eagle will make a nest at least eight feet by eight feet. (The largest on record was nine and a half feet wide, twenty feet deep, and weighed almost three *tons.*)

She will fill it up with leaves, animal fur, and down from her own breast, making a warm and cozy nest for her chicks. (Can you imagine how snug and safe those little guys felt at the bottom of that twenty-foot nest?) But when the time is right, she will start making things a bit uncomfortable for those unsuspecting little eaglets. It all begins when she takes them to a "home" that will be more important to them than any nest or aerie in the world…the sky! She will pick them up, take them in flight to a great and dizzying height, and *drop* them.

This is all shockingly new for the little eaglet. He's never flown a day in his life. For him, life has been a comfy, snuggled-down, fuzzball existence. A soft downy nest, little pals to play with, regular meals, and Mama's protective wings at night. But now Mama kicks him overboard and there is nothing between him and certain death but the wild blue yonder.

The eaglet begins to flutter. He's never done this before. He doesn't know what to do. He doesn't even have a learner's permit. His heart pounds in his tiny chest. And he's heading down, *fast.*

As the little fella plummets to earth, contemplating his comfortable but surprisingly brief life, Mama eagle watches. And what does she do? She swoops down just before her eaglet hits the ground, flies underneath, and picks him up. And of course the poor little bird has gone into cardiac arrest. But there's a happy ending here for the baby eagle, right? Mom is climbing back into the heavens. Oh boy, the nasty trauma is over. Back to the beloved nest…and isn't it just about lunchtime?

But what does she do when she regains her original altitude? She drops him again! And again! And each time she swoops down to save him and bears him up…on eagle's wings.

And that's exactly what the Lord is saying: "Moses, please tell them—make sure that you remind them—before you give them these commands, how much I have loved them in the past. Remind them how I've watched over their lives every day and concerned Myself about their future."

We can look back on the same thing in our own lives, can't we? Everything we have and everything we enjoy are because of Him and are blessings from His hand. We, too, were headed south one day. There was nothing between us and an eternal abyss but empty space and a long, long way to fall. As Paul put it, we were "without hope and without God in the world" (Ephesians 2:12, NIV).

But what happened? In Christ, the Lord swooped down and picked us up and gave us everything that we have. And now He sustains us and keeps us every day of our lives.

If we lose sight of that, we can't see anything at all.

Yes, there may be times when you feel abandoned like an eaglet in the wide, empty sky…but the Lord will always come. If you will trust Him and put your faith in Him, then He's guaranteed that He will always show up, and it will always be at the right time. If He seems "late" from your perspective, it's because He's letting you see something and learn something that you need to see and learn.

In their fishing boat out on the stormy sea, the disciples all thought they were going to die, that there was no hope. But Jesus came at just the right time, walking across the waves. He wouldn't have waited any longer, and He wouldn't have come any earlier.

Would the disciples have appreciated Him coming earlier, after they were straining at the oars for all those hours and their boat was being swamped and they were at the point of exhaustion and despair? Would they have preferred that He come earlier, before He met them at mid-lake? Yes, in their humanity they would have always preferred that. *But then they would not have known Him as Lord of the storm, Master of the waves and the sea. And Peter would not have learned that with his eyes on Jesus, he could overcome any obstacle or impossibility.*

Would Shadrach, Meshach, and Abednego have preferred that the Lord come swooping down to deliver them before King Nebuchadnezzar seized them, tied them up, and threw them into a fiery furnace? Yes, in their humanity they would have preferred that. *But then they would never have met the Fourth Man, standing with them in the flames. They would never have learned that the Lord could protect them from anything.*

God is all about developing us and helping us to grow. He loved the children of Israel, and His purpose was to lead them step by step, test by test, trial by trial, so that when they crossed the Jordan, they would have the faith and the strength and the confidence to throw down walled cities and take possession of the land. He always has a plan!

He has a plan for you, too. Never doubt it! You might be puzzled by the circumstances and timing in your life, and you may feel that you're going nowhere fast. Yet like that mother eagle, God's eye is upon you. He will catch you up on His wing and take you where you could never go in your own strength.

He carries you because He loves you. And that is what makes the Ten Commandments a love letter.

"FATHER KNOWS BEST"

The most meaningful book I've ever written had a very short print run.

Two copies.

But that's all right. I wouldn't have had it any other way.

The two copies went to the two young men I care about more than any young men on the face of this planet…my two sons, Ron Jr. and Mark. I gave them each a copy when they graduated from high school. It's a book that lists thirty critical life concerns and includes my convictions about faith, failure, success, love, relationships, money, prayer, and other topics close to this dad's heart.

It was no small task. The book represents many months of study, reflection, prayer, work—and a lifetime of experience. Joyce and I literally printed it ourselves and found a bookbinder in north Portland who lovingly bound it in leather and hand-stamped each cover in gold with the title "Father Knows Best."

Now why did I do that? Why did I take the trouble as a father to write such things to my sons? Why did I have the books typeset and printed and bound? Because I wanted this book packaged in such a way that Ron and Mark could take it with them and keep it with them over the long haul. I wanted to make sure that if they were ever confused or troubled in their minds or wondered what their dad might think or do in a given situation, they would at least have *something* to turn to. I wanted them to realize through the years that their dad cared enough about them and their futures to capture his heart for them in a book.

I felt such heaviness as I wrote, because my heart is so full of love for my boys. As I sat at my desk and penned these things onto a yellow pad, I found myself weeping over many of the pages. Why? Because I was pouring out my life for them…and because I knew my time with them under our roof was short. I knew they had grown up, and I wasn't going to get to be around them very much longer. They weren't going to be eating pancakes with me at the breakfast table or watching a ball game with me on TV in the family room.

And now they are gone.

Mark is married, with a home of his own, and Ron is engaged and busy in his work as a police officer. Sure, we still talk. We get together. We love doing things. But it isn't like it used to be…it can't be. Beyond that, my own health has left a question mark as to how long I'll even get to be there for them in an advisory role. There will come a day when they can't pick up the phone and ask me, "Dad, what do you think about this?" They won't be able to come into my office and say, "Well, Dad, how do you feel about that? What should I do?"

So I wanted it down on paper. I wanted to write it out with my own hands and personally place the book into *their* hands. I wanted to make sure they knew what their dad thought about some of these vital topics of life. I wanted to do all that I could do to remove confusion from their lives.

With all my heart, I want those young men to succeed.

With all my heart, I want those young men to escape the life-ravaging effects of sin.

With all my heart, I want those young men to grasp their destinies as sons of the living God.

Truthfully, it means the world to me to know they *have* kept these books close at hand. They've taken them to college. I've watched them pack the book in suitcases when they've gone on trips. I've been in their rooms at various times and seen the book on their dressers or nightstands.

I wrote with the thought that there might come a day when one of my sons would look at that book and say, "My dad wrote this. My dad put this together with his own hands. And he did it thinking about me, just because he loves me."

After all, this isn't a book of counsel from off the shelf or out of the blue. It isn't some ethics textbook from a faceless stranger. My sons have a context of *love* for these things. I've proven over and over again how much I love them. Everything I've said to them and done for them as a father from earliest memory stands as witness to the love behind my words of caution and instruction. They could never look at any chapter or any word in there and think anything but "My dad loves me. And if he loves me enough to put this down, I should pay attention to it."

Now tell me…could it be any less for God, the ultimate Father? What is His desire for our lives and our future? What is His heart toward His created ones? And what is the love I put into my little book compared to the infinite love God possesses for His sons and daughters? Isn't that what Jesus said? "If *you* know how to give good gifts to your children, how much more your heavenly Father!" (See Luke 11:13.)

In the book to my boys, I sketched out thirty areas of concern. God wrote down ten. I could have probably come up with fifty—or a hundred or a thousand—if I'd had the time, but God gave ten. And on reflection I've realized that everything I thought or wrote or could have written all fits somewhere under God's simple categories…His ten commandments.

I believe that God wrote what He wrote with His own hand for the same reason that I wrote to my boys. There are some things in this sin-damaged world of ours that are so shattering and devastating to our brief human lives that He doesn't want us to have to learn them by bitter experience. So He's given us His Word to guide us and protect us.

God knows there will be times in our lives when we will find ourselves in a lonely place, a dark place, a tight place, by ourselves, and we will wonder, "What should I do in this situation? What does my Father say about this? What's His heart in these matters? How does He feel about this?"

And God our Father—so much more than me, an imperfect human father—yearns for us to avoid destructive paths. So He gave us His Word, and specifically, He gave us the Ten Commandments.

He did it out of a heart of love,

wanting to remove confusion from our lives…

wanting to keep us from the traps and snares of the Destroyer…

wanting to spare us from the wasting, life-sapping ravages of sin…

wanting us to find our destiny as His own sons and daughters.

God knows that these truths are extremely important to our future. There are times when we become greatly confused about what is right and what is wrong, and about what we should and shouldn't do. This blurring of the lines is becoming more and more pronounced through our whole culture as the time of the Lord's coming draws near. What did Paul call these last days? "Perilous times" (2 Timothy 3:1). Terrible times. Difficult times. Grievous times. Dangerous times. And when we watch the news on TV or pick up a newspaper it should not surprise us that *no one seems to know what is right and ethical and moral anymore.*

No one can even agree on the ground rules. Our society's standards have been moved off their biblical foundations to rest on the shifting sands of public opinion polls...and as we all know, everyone has a different definition of right and wrong.

People say, "Well, this may be wrong for you, but it's right for me." Or "That may be wrong in this situation but may be right in that situation." Adultery? Lying? Stealing? How about killing? Aborting babies in the womb (we're told) is "compassionate and moral." Euthanizing old people in their final days is "compassionate and moral." Cloning human beings is "immoral" for now...but stay tuned. As it suits us, we may soon redefine that as "compassionate and moral," too.

When God wrote the Scriptures He knew very well what kind of world you and I and our children would be living in *right now.* It's no surprise to Him at all. He isn't shocked by any of it. He's omniscient. He knows exactly what we need to survive in this fast-changing, high-tech, low-morality culture we live in.

With the Ten Commandments, the Lord said, "Please...let

Me remove all confusion." In virtually every one of these commands, I find something of God's great protection and affection toward you and me. God says, "I know what is best for us, for you, for Me, for our relationship. There are some parameters here—ten of them—that are literally matters of life and death."

In all the confusion of our day, the Ten Commandments seem so simple and clear. Like big yellow warning signs on the highway.

I heard a story recently about Chi Chi Rodriguez, the famous golfer. He was driving down the street with his friend, going a lot faster than he should have been. A light changed from yellow to red up ahead of him, and he zoomed right through it. Didn't even slow down.

His friend almost had a coronary. He looked over at Chi Chi and sputtered, "Chi Chi, what in the world are you doing? You went right *through* a red light! Don't you stop for red lights?"

"My brother taught me to drive," Chi Chi replied, "and he doesn't stop for red lights. So I don't stop at red lights." And sure enough, a little farther down the road the pro golfer approached another intersection and blasted right through the red light.

His friend was a nervous wreck by then. "C'mon, man!" he said. "You're gonna get us *killed*. What in the world are you thinking of?"

Chi Chi repeated, "My brother taught me to drive, and he doesn't stop for red lights. So I don't stop at red lights."

Driving a little farther, they came to an intersection with a green light. This time, Chi Chi put on his brakes and stopped, nervously looking both ways.

"Why are you stopping *now?*" his friend asked. "This is a green light."

"I know," Chi Chi said. "My brother might be coming!"

We're all pretty accomplished at changing green lights into red lights and red lights into green lights, aren't we? Or maybe we'd rather that all of the lights were yellow, so we could look around quickly and keep on going the way we want to go. In other words, whatever you think or whatever you feel is fine, as long as you can get away with it and it doesn't do any immediate harm. But God understands the long-term *consequences* of disobedience...the consequences of life apart from His help and His blessing.

He can see the whole city map of our lives; He sees every intersection you will encounter for the rest of your life. And He knows that hurt and destruction and death await those who speed carelessly through life with scorn or apathy toward His Word. And *one wrong choice* can set us off on a road from which there is no easy return. Just a few days ago a young woman sat in my office, in despair over what had transpired in her life through addictions to heroin and crack. I said to her, "If you had it all to do over again, what would you do differently? Would you change anything?"

"Yeah," she said, looking up at me. "I came to a place in my life where I made a choice. It was like coming to a road and seeing a sign that said, 'Don't go down there'...but I went down there anyway. It's not difficult at all to realize exactly where it was that I made my mistake."

We've all made wrong turns. Some deliberately, some out of simple ignorance. The humbling fact is, you and I really don't understand much about life or the mysteries of life. When it comes right down to it, most of the time we just sort of blunder along in our brief three score and ten years, don't we? There are things we realize in our forties that we wish to goodness we had known in our twenties. There are things we finally understand in our sixties that would have been oh-so-helpful to have known in our thirties. Oh, how we need God's help! How we need God's Spirit! How we need God's loving guidelines. The truth is, we need help beyond our age or experience.

God, better than anyone else anywhere, understands how life works! The reason He gave us these commands is because He knows the consequences of each decision. He knows what the results will be of living without putting Him first.

I love it when the psalmist says, "Oh, how I love your law! I meditate on it all day long. Your commands make me wiser than my enemies, for they are ever with me. I have more insight than all my teachers, for I meditate on your statutes. I have more understanding than the elders, for I obey your precepts" (Psalm 119:97–100, NIV).

The psalmist is saying, "I have more wisdom and insight about life than by rights I really ought to have! I know how life works better than a man my age should really grasp, because I cling to the Word of God...I lean hard on His wisdom."

The Ten Commandments will keep us from destruction. Carefully heeding these ten warning signs in the power of the Holy Spirit will change the whole course of our lives. It will allow us to discover our very destiny as a child of God.

What do I mean by destiny? Just this. I believe that God has a vision for each one of us, for what we can be as we respond to Him and walk with Him. Isn't that what He was saying to Jeremiah?

"For I know the plans I have for you," declares the LORD, "plans to prosper you and not to harm you, plans to give you hope and a future." (Jeremiah 29:11, NIV)

He knows what we can *become* in Him as we are obedient. He doesn't want us to miss that opportunity. He holds it out before us, and He knows that His commandments, as we are enabled to live in them by the power of His indwelling Son, point the way toward that future. (See Philippians 3:12–14.)

Do you remember this familiar passage from Isaiah?

"For My thoughts are not your thoughts,
Nor are your ways My ways," says the LORD.
"For as the heavens are higher than the earth,
So are My ways higher than your ways,
And My thoughts than your thoughts."
(Isaiah 55:8–9)

What does God mean here? That He's smarter than us? Well, obviously! I think that in the context of this passage, He's giving us a very different message…a message of hope.

I hear the Lord saying, "Because of what you've experienced and where you are in your life's journey, you don't believe in *you*. You don't think there's any hope for you. You don't think there's any destiny for you. You don't think there's any chance or any future for you." And I believe He is saying to us, "You ought to be very thankful that I don't think about you the way *you* think about you. My plans for you are greater than yours could ever be! I do have a destiny and purpose for you. I do have things

31

planned for you—even though you don't think you could ever be anything or accomplish anything or do anything. You say in your heart, 'After what I've been and what I've done, God could never use me.' But I can! And I will, as you obey Me and allow Me to indwell you through My Holy Spirit."

His heart and His thoughts toward you are greater than your own heart and thoughts toward you. You look at yourself, and by your evaluation you're washed up, passed up, beat up, and mostly used up. But your thoughts about you are too small!

There is no way for you to even comprehend the good things God has in store for you. What He wants to do with you. The way He wants to use you. The way He wants to bless you. And He gave you the Ten Commandments to keep you from destruction so that you could enter into all He desires for you. In other words, the Lord says, "I have a great destiny for you. I have dreams and plans for you. Won't you walk in my ways and choose to obey and follow Me?" As Moses said to the children of Israel as they were about to enter the land, *choose life.*

My sons have my heart and my counsel for them between the pages of a little leather book. But far greater than that, they have the counsel of their heavenly Father in His Book—words from Someone who loves them more than I ever could.

I've talked to a number of my friends, and almost all of them can remember getting letters and cards and notes from their mothers through the years. But that number dwindles very rapidly when you begin talking about fathers! The reaction to a letter from a dad is sometimes "Who died?" or "Whoa, this is a major event. Something big must have happened."

Something big *has* happened. Your Father took time to

write, and it was such an important letter that He literally wrote it with His own hand…the very finger of God (Exodus 31:18).

He wanted to make sure that in those times when we long for counsel about which way to turn, we'd know just what to do.

The best turn is always a turn toward Him.

Your Father knows best.

HOW SHOULD I RESPOND?

As I write these words, February 14 draws nigh on my calendar.

Unless you're Charlie Brown or Saddam Hussein, you've probably given and received some special valentines in your life. You've probably had some things wrapped in red foil or fancy ribbon or a heart-shaped box. Or maybe you've stood at a florist's counter, trying to decide on a "just right" arrangement of roses.

It's fun to say "I love you" in elegant, ornamental ways sometimes. It's fun to bring a sparkle of surprise into the eyes of your valentine. (Even a Snickers bar looks better if it's got a red ribbon around it.)

But the truth is, love doesn't always come wrapped that way. Love doesn't always arrive in pink foil with little red hearts. It doesn't always come in a perfect bouquet of hothouse flowers.

Love comes in surprising packages sometimes. Love—the real thing—arrives at the front porch of your life in ways you might not expect or immediately recognize. You have to have your eyes open to see it…and receive it.

It may come in a normally reserved father's quick tear.

Or in a teenaged son's spontaneous, awkward hug.

Or in a little girl's crayoned landscape, created just for you.

Or in a friend's quiet willingness to put his or her own shoulder under your too-heavy load.

Or on a lonely, blood-soaked cross one dark Friday, somewhere outside the city gates.

Love doesn't always look the way you'd expect it to look. It isn't always dressed for dinner. It isn't always pretty or frilly or soft. It might even be written in stone.

It might even show up as Ten Commandments.

I have come to believe that the Ten Commandments are one of the greatest pieces of literature concerning the love of God that there is anywhere. People say, "Are you kidding? They're tough, demanding, and requiring. How in the world can you say that these commands have anything to do with the love of God?"

As I've already mentioned, I believe it because of what God does in the first nineteen chapters of the book of Exodus *prior* to the Ten Commandments. As you read this brief history of the infant nation, you can't help but notice that every time they are in trouble and every time they are in a difficult place, the Lord's always there. He's always there to help them. He's always there to deliver them. He's always there to see them through.

So, if the Lord loved them and proved it by His care and concern, then why in the world would He turn from being a serving, sustaining, and giving God to a selfish, demanding, do-it-my-way-or-else kind of God? Why in the world should we see the Ten Commandments as anything but a tender love letter?

The Lord didn't want to bind His people in leg shackles and chains after gloriously redeeming them from the death angel and releasing them from slavery. Would He bear them on eagles' wings to a prison? What sort of deliverance would that be? God knew that all of these commands He set before them, every one of them, would bring about blessing, life, peace, and a secure future. His commandments were (and are) a gift of love in an uncertain and dangerous world.

How then should you respond to such a gift?

One of the best ways I can think of is to *prepare yourself* to hear Him.

Before the Lord gave the Ten Commandments, He told Moses, "I am going to come to you in the form of a dark cloud, so that the people themselves can hear me when I talk with you. Go down now and see that the people are ready for my visit… Sanctify them today and tomorrow, and have them wash their clothes. Then, the day after tomorrow, I will come down upon Mt. Sinai as all the people watch" (Exodus 19:9, 10–11, TLB).

So Moses did just that. He told the people, "Get ready for God's appearance two days from now" (Exodus 19:15, TLB).

The Lord makes an issue of preparing to receive these commandments, doesn't He? What does God tell them to do? Wash your clothes. Take a little time to get ready; this is important stuff. When God comes down to visit your camp, you want to be prepared. He told them specifically how He wanted them to meet Him.

In other words, this is going to require something of you. A seriousness of purpose. An attitude that says, "Okay, God, let's do business. I want my life to be right. I want to hear everything that You have to say to me." You approach such a moment with God reverently, expectantly, humbly, carefully, and with a sense of awe.

How do you and I prepare ourselves for something God might like to give to us or say to us—even in the pages of this book? As I thought about that, a vision of my garage came to mind. I don't know what your garage looks like. Ours is looking better, for once, because we spent a full day mucking it out. Why did we bother with that? For the simple reason that we would like to be able to put something in there...like a car. (Now there's a novel thought.) But before we deposit something so large and important IN the garage, we have to clean a lot of clutter OUT of the garage.

In the same way, you can't have God's best, you can't have the fulfillment of His promise in your life, until you come to the realization, "I need to be available. I need to make room in my life for Him. I need to prepare my heart to receive whatever it is He wants to give to me."

Is there clutter in your life that keeps you from receiving from Him? If God wanted to communicate something deeply personal to your heart this afternoon...would you even be prepared to hear Him? Would you be able to receive the message?

What does "clutter" consist of? It would certainly include those things Jesus listed in the parable of the sower, where faith is "choked out by worry and riches and the responsibilities and pleasures of life" (Luke 8:14, TLB).

The clutter also must include unconfessed sin. Moses told

the people to wash their clothes…we need to have our heart and conscience washed clean. David prayed, "Search me, O God, and know my heart; try me, and know my anxieties; and see if there is any wicked way in me, and lead me in the way everlasting" (Psalm 139:23–24).

It's a great prayer, because God very much *wants* to "lead you in the way everlasting." Sin in your life doesn't stop God from giving, it just stops you from receiving. God is a giving and loving God; that doesn't change. But our ability to receive His love and counsel are frustrated and blocked by unconfessed sin. Adam and Eve are a good illustration of this. They sinned, but God kept His appointment with them. He came at the usual time "in the cool of the day" to enjoy fellowship and companionship with them, but they were crouching somewhere out in the woods! He was still coming to love them, to talk with them, to give to them, but they had removed themselves. They were no longer in a position to receive. They hid from Him, first behind the bushes, and then behind their excuses.

Preparing to meet with Him and receive from Him means coming out of hiding. It means opening our hearts to His divine inspection. It means agreeing with Him about the sin in our lives. And what is sin? Yes, it is falling short of His standards, but I also think it means trying in my own strength to fulfill my own needs. It's where we say, "I don't need God in this, I'll do this myself."

The Bible tells us, "If we say we have no sin, we are only fooling ourselves and refusing to accept the truth. But if we confess our sins to him, he is faithful and just to forgive us and to cleanse us from every wrong" (1 John 1:8–9, NLT).

In Moses' day, the emphasis was on obedience to a God they greatly feared but hardly knew. A God who came down upon a mountain in a dark cloud with earthquakes and flashes of lightning. In our day, this wonderful day of grace, we come to a God we know, the Son of God who lived and died for us and now pleads our case before His Father's throne. How can we *not* want to prepare ourselves to meet and listen to such a God? How can we satisfy ourselves with anything less than making room for all He wants to give to us and say to us?

The old apostle John understood this truth very well when he wrote: "Loving God means doing what he tells us to do, and really, that isn't hard at all; for every child of God can obey him, defeating sin and evil pleasure by trusting Christ to help him" (1 John 5:3–4, TLB).

It's a lot easier now for me to look at these Ten Commandments and to remind myself, "Lord, why would I ever doubt Your love for me? You have proven it over and over again. You even wrote it down."

It was a valentine written in stone. Later, it would be written in blood. Who could question such a love as that?

And God spoke all these words,
saying: "I am the LORD your God,
who brought you out of the land of Egypt,
out of the house of bondage.
You shall have no other gods before Me."

EXODUS 20:1–3

~∾∽~

CHAPTER 2

NO OTHER GODS

The greatest challenge in all of life is to keep Him first.

I'm often asked, "What's the hardest thing about being a pastor of a large church? What is the greatest burden you feel in the ministry? Preaching? Counseling? Administering?"

My answer has to be, "None of the above."

While any one of these tasks can be daunting or demanding on any given day, there is something even more difficult than these. As a matter of fact, I could be dazzling everyone every week with my sermons, saving marriages every day in counseling, and administering a staff and budget the size of the Pentagon's, and *still* be a miserable failure in my Lord's eyes.

The greatest challenge I face every day of my life is probably the very one that you face every day…maintaining a close, personal, growing relationship with Jesus Christ. It is keeping Him first.

Our number-one task as believers is to make sure that nothing—no "god," person, object, task, duty, or pleasure—comes before Him in our priorities, in our plans, and in our affection.

This is no small thing! The good folks in the church at Ephesus worked extremely hard, kept their hopes alive, stayed doctrinally sound, and patiently endured suffering for the Lord's name. Yet the Lord Jesus said they were on the razor-edge of losing both their light and their witness in the world. Why? Because "you have left your first love" (Revelation 2:4).

Hard work and good teaching and a willingness to stand in the gap for the Lord aren't enough. This is a *relationship,* and the Lord is very, very concerned with the condition of our hearts toward Him.

King Solomon would have known the first command from boyhood. And I would guess it was very much on his mind when he wrote these words: "Trust in the LORD with all your heart and lean not on your own understanding; in all your ways acknowledge him, and he will make your paths straight" (Proverbs 3:5–6, NIV).

"All of our ways" means all of our opportunities and undertakings. The word "acknowledge" doesn't mean just to "know" Him by studying *about* Him, but rather through a personal relationship *with* Him. *The Living Bible* paraphrases it like this: "In everything you do, put God first, and he will direct you and crown your efforts with success."

That's pretty much the bottom line, isn't it? In *everything* you do, put God first, so He can direct your path. So what does that mean? It means He not only gives you direction, but He commits Himself to removing any hindrances or obstacles that stand in the way of His destined purpose for you. He will make the path straight before you.

But notice that this statement is conditional. It tells us very specifically that *we must not lean on or trust in our own understanding.* Why? Because that understanding is so inadequate, limited, and flawed by sin. Here we are on a broken planet, a world under God's curse. We are in a dangerous place full of traps and pits and bottomless swamps…and our compass is broken! How can we move forward at all into life without moving into disaster? We cannot rely on our own wisdom or sense of direction. The Bible says, "There is a way which seems right to a man, but its end is the way of death" (Proverbs 14:12).

I was in New England recently, speaking to a group of pastors at a retreat center out in a wilderness area. It was very cold, and we'd just experienced a major snowstorm. One beautiful, moonlit night, one of the pastors slipped out of bed, put on some snowshoes, and headed off into the woods for a walk. He went alone, with no flashlight or compass or provisions of any sort.

He never marked his trail, never looked at his watch, and paid no attention to landmarks. After a couple hours of wandering in the still, silver moonlight, he suddenly realized he was becoming very, very cold. And in that same instant he was jarred by another realization: "I'm lost! I have no idea how to get back!"

He certainly hadn't planned on getting lost. He just wasn't thinking. For some reason, he had a false sense of confidence that he could easily find his way back in the dark. But he couldn't. Others had to search for him in the night and the bitter cold, and they eventually found him…cold, embarrassed, but none the worse for his midnight wanderings.

That's the deceptiveness of the path that the world offers. It looks good, it looks inviting, it seems fine, until it suddenly dawns on you: "I don't know where I am! I've wandered into something and have no idea how to go back or get out of this." You're lost in the woods at night. You're out in the cold, and it's too dark to follow your own tracks home.

Those without the guidance of God's Word and God's Spirit—for all of their sincerity or lofty motives or desire to be good people and good parents and good citizens—will walk into heartache after heartache, disaster after disaster. They can't help it! As Jesus said, "They are blind guides leading the blind, and both will fall into a ditch" (Matthew 15:14, TLB).

Yes, but these commands of God…don't they have a "stern" quality about them that—well, puts us off sometimes? Isn't that our first reaction when we hear someone even mention the Ten Commandments? And yet, when you are warning someone not to venture down a path where certain death awaits, how stern do you get?

Imagine you are on a family vacation at Yosemite National Park, and you take the long, winding drive up to Glacier Point. A short walk from the parking lot brings you to the top of a sheer rock cliff, where you can peer over a belt-high railing straight down at the valley about 3,200 feet below. The car doors fling open and before you can even get your seat belt unlatched, Tommy, your excited three-year-old, leaps out of the car and begins running for the edge as fast as his chubby little legs will carry him.

Is it a time to whisper sweetly? Is it a time to speak quietly and softly? Is it a time for a seminar on "values clarification"? No! As your parent's heart lurches within your chest, you shout, "Tommy, *stop!* STOP RIGHT NOW!"

Do the Ten Commandments have a bit of that flavor to them? Do they seem to be written in bold with capital letters? Could it be because the Father heart of God lurches within Him as He sees spiritually blind, unheeding men and women running for the edge of the cliff? Listen to the urgent tone of these words from the book of Ezekiel:

> "As surely as I live, declares the Sovereign LORD, I take no pleasure in the death of the wicked, but rather that they turn from their ways and live. Turn! Turn from your evil ways! Why will you die, O house of Israel?" (Ezekiel 33:11, NIV)

Can you hear it? *"Stop! Stop! Turn back! Turn around! Don't go that way! There is sorrow ahead! There is death ahead! Come back to Me."*

It's as if the Lord was saying, "If you will acknowledge Me in all your ways, if you will hear and obey My word, I'll show you a blessed path. What's more, I will keep you from harm and let nothing get in the way of your fulfillment." So the closer I get to His words and His commands, the more I acknowledge His first place in my life, the closer I get to His desire and purposes for me.

Why in the world does He make such a point of having no other gods before Him? What does this first command have to do with life in today's world?

The reason is very simple: He wants to be your God.

He wants to care for you, and He knows that no one or nothing can care for you better than He. He is a faithful God, committed to us even when we fail, even when we make mistakes. He loves us, and He will never say, "I'm done with you. I'm going to turn to someone else that I care about more than you."

Psalm 116 says that when I call upon Him in my sorrows and distress, He *inclines* unto me. He leans over to listen to me. He turns aside from His present work to help you and me. No matter where He's working or what project He's involved in, He hears us call and turns to help us. The psalmist was so overwhelmed by God's goodness that he wanted to express it, and so he wrote this psalm…a psalm of love.

In verse 13 he says, "I will take up the cup of salvation, and call upon the name of the LORD." This word "salvation" is not a reference to being saved as we mean it today; Old Testament believers didn't understand salvation as we do in the shadow of the cross. It was rather a reference to the many times the Lord had salvaged him, helped him, sustained him, and saved him from trouble and grief. His life was full and overflowing with God's goodness.

I have a cup like that, too. And in this cup of salvation are the many times God has helped me overcome doubt, disappointment, and failure. The times when He spared my life, kept our children from danger, protected us from rash, foolish decisions, and paid our bills. He's been so good. He has loved us and reached out to us and delivered us even when we were unlovely. He has made such a commitment to us in His love. And now He is saying, "Would it be asking too much—knowing that I love you with a sacrificial, serving love—would you consider making Me the most important thing in your life? Would you consider Me as first in your life, just as you are first in Mine?"

He is saying, "Please don't invest your life in those fleeting, temporary distractions that surround you. Don't turn to the world for satisfaction, fulfillment, and quick-fix remedies for a wounded heart. Those things aren't going to bring blessing and prosperity to your life. They will turn to ashes in your hands, and leave you even more empty and disappointed than before."

What happens, then, when I do make sure that He is first in my life?

It changes destructive worry and anxiety patterns in my mind. Where I once became locked up with fear, I now have confidence.

In the day when I am afraid,
I will have confidence in Thee.
(Psalm 56:3, MLB)

Many people ask me how I've dealt with years of leukemia—years of hanging by a rope over the edge of a cliff. My answer might be that it's not so bad when you know who is holding the rope! I've settled into a sense of confidence that my time is in the Lord's hands. Please, hear me on this: *my life really is His responsibility.* Because of that, I don't worry, because He's going to care for everything. Scripture says, "You can throw the whole weight of your anxieties upon Him, for you are His personal concern" (1 Peter 5:7, Phillips). When you put Him first and He's everything to you, that's what you've done.

He is responsible for my life. He is responsible for the outcome. He is responsible for how long I live and how long I get to serve and minister. The weight of it is off my shoulders. He's responsible for what happens in the end—*and I'm not!* I just get to enjoy the journey.

In fact, I believe it is what you *don't* surrender that ends up eating you alive, because you carry it and feel so responsible to somehow bring it all to a good conclusion—when deep in your heart you know you never can.

What does Jesus say so clearly in Matthew 6? "Don't worry. Don't worry about anything. Don't worry about what you're going to eat. Don't worry about what you're going to drink. Don't worry about what you're going to wear or where you're going to live. Don't fret over those things at all. Just be sure to seek Me first, and everything will work out for the best."

Worry is like a red warning light on the dashboard, informing us that we are not putting God first in our lives. It alerts us that we've taken back our lives from His care—a very foolish and even dangerous thing to do.

Again, what happens when I make sure that He is first in my life?

It will make an impact on the people around me. You cannot put God first in your life and avoid notice. People can't help but sense something different about you, because of the way you operate under stress and pressure and the way you view material things. The world will wonder how and why you respond the way you do. (What's with this guy? Is he in a daze? What's the story with this lady? Can she be for real?) Peter foresaw a day when you will be questioned about that mysterious, calming, invisible component in your life.

> But in your hearts set apart Christ as Lord. Always be prepared to give an answer to everyone who asks you to give the reason for the hope that you have. But do this with gentleness and respect. (1 Peter 3:15, NIV)

Set apart Christ as Lord in your heart. That's another way of saying, *Keep Him first.* And really, when you stop to think about it, why should we NOT want to put Him first?

I love the story I heard about an eight-year-old boy who sat in class, taking a test. He became so nervous and distraught about completing the test on time that he suddenly wet his pants. Horrors! He looked down and saw a little puddle there beneath him. Sick with worry and embarrassment, he looked up just in time to see his teacher motioning him to her desk. But how could he move? What would he do? Noticing that the boy seemed frozen in his chair, the teacher got up from her desk and began walking down the aisle toward him. *Oh no!* he groaned to himself. *What in the world am I going to do now? She's going to see this puddle and everybody will laugh. It's going to be horrible.*

What he didn't know was at that very moment one of his classmates, a little girl, was coming down the aisle from behind him carrying a large fishbowl. When she got up alongside him, she suddenly lurched and dropped the heavy bowl. It shattered with a loud crash and sent water, broken glass, and displaced fish flying everywhere. Now covered by fish-tank water, the boy sat there thinking, *Thank God! Thank God! There IS a God in heaven! What a wonderful gift! What a wonderful girl!*

But then it dawned on him that little boys don't even like little girls. He couldn't possibly let the incident pass. He looked at her and said, "What's wrong with you, you clumsy clod? Can't you watch where you're going?!" As the class laughed at the girl, the teacher took the boy (now covered by dignity) to the gym class to get him some dry clothes to wear.

At lunchtime, no one wanted to sit with the girl. Her friends avoided her at recess. In the unforgiving society of elementary school, she was suddenly a plague and a pariah.

When the day was over and the boy was on his way home, he walked out the door and saw her. All the kids were leaving, but she was walking by herself, along the fence. He began to reflect on what had happened that day and suddenly—on an impulse—walked over to her.

"You know," he said, "I've been thinking about what happened today. That wasn't an accident, was it? You did that on purpose, didn't you?"

"Yes," she said. "I did do it on purpose. I knew what had…happened to you. You see, I wet my pants once, too."

I heard this story and thought, "Lord, I don't want to ever forget what You have done for me. I, too, have wet my pants. But You covered me. You spilled Your precious blood for me and covered my sins. You took all of my shame upon Yourself. Now I'm clean. You have fit me for heaven, even though I deserved hell. You saw my hopeless situation and rescued me. You have given me dignity and hope and a reason to get out of bed in the morning."

Why should I ever want to put anyone or anything in front of Him? Why should I tolerate other gods in my life? Why should I look for other saviors? Why should I serve lesser lords? He promised to provide for me everything I need. My life has completely changed, so why not tell the whole world what a mess I was in when He found me? But Jesus came along and took away my embarrassment and shame. Oh, how I love Him. That's the reason we can hold out hope for others. That's the reason we can say, "Put God first and He'll cover your past. If God has forgiven me, He can forgive you."

How could I *not* want to put such a God first?

Lord, I praise You as the all-powerful, all-knowing, every-where-present God of the universe. What really touches me is that You control all things for my good! You made me for Yourself, and it moves me to think You would choose me for a committed love relationship. You have proven Your faithfulness to me so many times and in so many ways. Why would I ever seek another god who would be so grossly inadequate in comparison to You?

And so today, Lord, give me the grace to love You every day as You have loved me. In Jesus' name, amen.

"You shall not make for yourself a carved image—
any likeness of anything that is in heaven above,
or that is in the earth beneath,
or that is in the water under the earth;
you shall not bow down to them nor serve them.
For I, the LORD *your God, am a jealous God."*

EXODUS 20:4–5

❦

CHAPTER 3

PURSUING
EMPTY IMAGES

WHOSE PICTURE IN
MY WALLET?

Have I mentioned that I love my wife Joyce very, very much?

I really do. We've been married for over thirty years now, and I'm as delighted with her today as I was when I was a Bible college preacher boy with stars in my eyes.

But tell me…how do you think she would like it if she saw my billfold lying open on our dresser some morning and noticed a picture of another attractive woman alongside her picture? Do you think she would shrug her shoulders and say, "Well, this is interesting, but after all, Ron has a right to his privacy"? Or do you think it more likely she might walk into the bathroom where I'm shaving and say, "Ron, who is *this?*"

And how do you think she would like it if she learned that this other woman and I had a bit of an ongoing relationship— that I turned to her when I felt especially in need of support, affection, and encouragement? Do you think that might bother Joyce at all? Do you think she would continue to believe me when I whisper in her ear that I love her with all of my heart?

Do you think she would have any reason to feel a little revulsion toward that image in my wallet? Could you really blame her if she wanted to confront me or tear that photograph into a few hundred pieces? Could you fault her for feeling jealous or hurt or angry over having to share my love and devotion with another?

Dumb question, huh? *She's my wife.* She has every right to expect and even insist that I keep myself for her and her alone. And you know what? I want to. Because of my love for her, and my vows to her, I've always been a one-woman man.

I believe this to be the very spirit of the second commandment. Here's my sense of what the Lord is saying: "I am your God. I am your Redeemer. I have saved you and bought you for Myself at a terrible price. Please...don't ever put anything in the place that belongs to Me. I love you with all My heart, and I've always wanted to care for you, protect you, provide for you, and bless you. Now—because I love you more than any other—let Me ask something very important to Me. I'm asking that you have no other gods in your life...that I would be the only One."

What do you think? Does this strike you as a little too restrictive? Too legalistic? Too much for the Lord to expect or require? Of course not. *He is our God.* After all, what's the difference between a "carved image" or "graven image" and a photograph? Isn't He saying something like this to you and me? "Listen, do you have any idea how much I love you, and how much you mean to Me? Please...don't put any other pictures in your billfold alongside Mine. Don't carry any other images in your heart. Don't turn to any false god for comfort, stimulation, or heart satisfaction. Here I am! I am able to meet your every need."

It's a love issue. It's a relationship issue. My wife doesn't want any rivals for my love. My Lord doesn't, either. His heart toward you and me does not change through the seasons and the years. What of our heart toward Him?

Every now and then, I hear a man or woman utter some horrible words in my office. It's like a body blow each time I hear them. "Pastor, I just don't love my wife anymore." Or "I don't love my husband anymore." When that happens, I always ask myself, *Why? How could it happen? How could that be? What do they even mean by the word 'love'?*

In fact, I've been so troubled by this situation that I've changed the way I do premarital counseling. It's very typical for a couple to come into my office all calf-eyed, lovey-dovey, and wrapped about one another like two vines of ivy. They can't seem to keep their hands or their eyes off each other, and I'm not sure they're really hearing much of what I have to say. In recent days, I've been spoiling the party attitude by making them sit on opposite ends of the couch.

I want them to understand that this business of pledging your very life to another is no dance through the daisies. It is very, very serious. Once I get them untwined and separated, I'll turn to the young man, look him straight in the eyes, and say, "Will you love this woman and serve her and care for her for the rest of your life? Are you prepared *right now* to say that the only thing you want out of this relationship is to fulfill her, build her up, and satisfy her? Are you willing *this moment* to release your expectations? Are you ready to say that the whole reason you are marrying this woman is because you believe you are God's gift to her, blessing and caring for her?"

Now, this isn't usually what the young man is expecting. Some of the color drains out of his face as the realization and weight of what he's doing begins to sink in.

He swallows hard. "Yes, Pastor," he croaks.

But I'm not done with him yet.

I will say, "Now, if you know that this is the will of God, and that you're entering into this relationship not to receive anything, but to give everything, then *I want you to remember this day.* I don't want you coming to me five years from now telling me you 'don't love her.' Because I will know that you certainly *did* love her, and love isn't something you can junk or trade in after a few years and fifty thousand miles like a used car. And I don't want you coming to me saying, 'This wasn't the will of God,' because we're sitting here today and we know that it certainly *is* the will of God."

It's a very sobering moment. These couples are hardly ever prepared for that sort of direct language. But I want them to understand that this relationship is for *life.*

And our relationship with the Lord is for life, too—and life beyond life. The commitment we make to Him is an eternal commitment, and God takes it very seriously. Might not God be saying to us something like this? "I'm committed to you and you alone. I would never leave you and run to another. Would you please do one thing? Don't put anything between you and Me. Don't carry other images close to your heart. Don't surrender My place to another."

The elderly apostle John, writing to believers toward the end of his life, said: "Little children, keep yourselves from idols" (1 John 5:21). What was he talking about? A hunk of metal? A statue chipped out of stone? Wasn't he talking about something more?

Matthew Henry explains: "Since you know the true God, and are in Him, let your light and love guard you against all that is advanced in opposition to Him, or competition with Him.... Cleave to Him in faith, and love, and constant obedience, *in opposition to all things that would alienate your mind and heart from God.*"

What then are those "images" in our world today that would rise up to challenge our love relationship with the Son of God? What are the snapshots we might be tempted to frame on our desk, alongside the picture of Him? What are those "pictures in our wallet" that could gradually steal us away from a whole-hearted walk with Christ?

Material things, maybe? Jesus said to His disciples, "You cannot serve both God and Money" (Matthew 6:24, NIV). He was speaking in that instance of a spirit of materialism that grips the soul and demands our energies and devotion. Paul says in Colossians 3:5 that even greediness is idolatry. But Scripture might have also listed any of the other gods of this world—false images such as Power, or Pleasure, or Fame, or Status.

When it becomes the whole purpose of my life to chase one of those images, I have already slipped into idolatry. I have given it the best of my time, my talents, my treasures, and my energies. My very life is *invested* in it. That's what a god is; when you worship a god, you basically surrender your life to it.

In the book of Acts, Paul was bewildered by the "many

gods" that filled the city of Athens. From his perspective, there must have been an idol of some kind on every block—as regular as downtown fire hydrants. But what is that in comparison with today? Today, these gods of materialism, sexual indulgence, and personal power fill the very airwaves! The images and their deceptive offers go across the world by satellite, cable, Internet, and slick four-color printing. We are *surrounded* by more images than we have ever been in the history of the world. They leer at us from billboards and magazine covers. They call to us in powerful visual impressions on television. And as every good advertising or network executive knows, the whole object is to absolutely "capture" as many people as possible.

Capture what? Our attention. Our interest. Our money. Our time. Our commitment. Is there anything wrong with wanting a new car? Is there anything wrong with wanting to wear attractive, fashionable clothing? Is there anything wrong with wanting to succeed in business? Is there anything wrong with being a loyal sports fan? No. But any of these things—or a hundred others—may become an idol to us as it begins to control our thoughts and desires.

How do those false images affect us over the long haul? This is where Scripture makes some amazing—even frightening—statements.

Psalm 135 tells us:

The idols of the nations are but silver and gold, the work of man's hands. They have mouths, but they do not speak; they have eyes, but they do not see; they have ears, but they do not hear; nor is there any breath at all in their mouths. *Those who make them will be like them, yes, everyone who trusts in them.* (Psalm 135:15–18, NASB)

In other words, I will become just like that image I pursue. This is profound truth. The Lord says the same thing to the prophet Jeremiah: "What fault did your fathers find in me, that they strayed so far from me? They followed worthless idols and became worthless themselves" (Jeremiah 2:5, NIV). Another translation says, "They went far from Me and walked after emptiness and became empty" (NASB).

The clear fact is, we become like that which we worship. And God knows this. He knows the hollow despair that follows such a life. He knows that these false images will never satisfy my deeper thirsts or the longings of my heart. As Jesus said to the woman at the well, If you drink this water, you'll just be thirsty again. You'll have to come every day for more, and you'll never be satisfied. But there is a well—a well of living water—that could keep you from ever being thirsty again.

The Lord knows that in time I will discover that those things that are worthless in the eyes of God will cause me to feel the same way: worthless, drained of value.

I will be left empty-handed and broken.

Not long ago I watched a commercial on television that brought it all home to me. Maybe you've seen it, too. A very impressive, handsome young man is standing alongside the road, hitchhiking. His shirt is open to the chest, his hair looks casually disarranged—like a model's. He's standing out in the barren desert in the heat of the day, calm as can be, with his thumb out.

Out of nowhere, you hear the whine of a sports car. It's a red one, of course, with a beautiful woman at the wheel. She speeds right on by the hitchhiker in a cloud of dust, seeming to ignore his existence. Then something apparently hits her, because she jams on the brakes, throws the car into reverse, and backs up to where the young man is standing. With a manicured finger on the window button, she lowers the glass and looks up at him over the top of her Foster Grants. He leans down to look inside.

"Are those *Bugle Boy* jeans?" she asks.

By now his heart is pumping a mile a minute. He's ready to climb into the car with this vision of beauty, sure that she'll take him into never-never land.

"Why yes," he replies, "they are."

The lady nods and says, "Thank you." Up goes the window, down goes the accelerator, and off she goes in another billow of dust, the sound of the sports car fading in the desert hills.

When I first saw that commercial, I thought, what a tremendous (although perhaps unintended) illustration of the image makers of our world. They say, "Wear our stuff. Listen to our music. Talk like us. Look like us. Dance to our dance." And while you're investing your time and spending your resources and trying so very hard to achieve that elusive "right look," the world is going to leave you standing alone alongside the road with nothing.

God knows all about that, too. He knows that when I pursue those things, they'll leave me empty-handed and unfulfilled. He knows that somewhere along the line, I'll find myself jilted by these false lovers. I'll be left standing alongside the road in some barren, thirsty place. The guy in the commercial bought into the idea that he could look so cool, so desirable, that he could make this beauty in the sports car pick him up. And it did make her stop. It did make her notice. But he didn't get the girl, and he didn't get a ride. All he got was a look. He was left alone with unfulfilled expectations…and a face full of desert dust.

Our Father knows that the "images" offered by the world are bankrupt. He knows that if we pursue them, in the end we will find ourselves disappointed, devastated, and worthless because of what we've experienced. The false gods will only take, take, take.

Just yesterday I was talking with a young woman in my office. She sat on the couch, weeping, hands covering her face. "I've lost everything," she said, looking up at me with red, swollen eyes. "I've lost my virginity. I've lost my sense of value. Look at all these holes!" To gain the acceptance of her peers, she had pierced herself for multiple rings in her ears and nose and mouth. "I'm twenty-one years old," she said, "and I'm just tired. I don't want to live like this anymore. I thought—I thought it was going to be so good."

Scripture tells us that the gods of this world will lead us astray. They will lead us where God really doesn't want us to go. They will use us up, drain us dry, and then discard us. What did that verse say? The gods of this world have feet…but they can't come to you when you are in need. They have hands…but they won't lift a finger to help you when you're struggling. They have eyes…but they don't see your heart or what's going on in your life. They have ears…but don't hear you cry out when you are lonely or frightened or in despair.

What this young woman was saying was, "Everything I

wanted and reached for was just a sham. Now look at me. Why would anyone love me? Who could ever love me?" And sitting there with her in my office yesterday afternoon, I had the privilege of telling her about someone who really did love her very much. Someone worthy of her faith and devotion. Someone who loved her just the way she was. Someone who would never use her and abandon her. Someone who would one day make her shine like a star in the heavens with His reflected beauty and righteousness (Philippians 2:15–16).

"Honey," I said, "I'm just so thrilled that we got to talk today, because I'm going through a study on the Ten Commandments. You know, you think there's not a chance in the world for you, and that there's no hope at all. But can I tell you what God did for Israel? He loved them so much that when they were in deep trouble, He swooped right down like a mama eagle and picked them up. He blessed them and graced their lives, and He can do the same for you. Just as sure as when you were born your mother had great plans for you, so God Himself loves you so much that right now, even in your failure, He wants to come and touch your life and give you a hope for tomorrow."

False images will always deceive you.

People who are sold out to status and fashion and an expensive lifestyle really do look great! They seem to have absolutely everything. But when life begins to press in on them, there is nothing on the inside to hold them up. There's no structure. No framework. No foundation. Nothing beneath the image. When the pressure comes (as it always will) these men and women will collapse like a deflated balloon.

I have a mental picture at this moment of the back lot at

Paramount Studios. If you're on a tour, you can see the street of some little town, with the stores and courthouse and shops and churches. But they're only false fronts. They look great in a movie but if you tried, for instance, to go into the dry goods store, you'd walk through a door into the sand and weeds. There's nothing there. No store. No dry goods. No people. Nothing but a dusty, garbage-strewn back lot. There's nothing to eat, no place to live, no place to stay, no place to worship. It's empty.

What's really depressing is that you walk down one of the streets, and everything is just like you remember it on TV or in the movies. But then when they drive you around the corner, you see that it's all make-believe. There's nothing behind those building fronts but trash. They've thrown everything back there, because nobody ever sees it—rusted-out cars and barrels and the collected junk of many years.

The world's false images set up the same kind of deception. They promise one thing, they call to the emotions, they look so desirable, they weave a beautiful dream, but when you get into them, you end up with a big handful of nothing.

The world says, "You can be anything and look like anything that you want to. If you give us time, we can reshape you." The media says, "Image is everything." Listen, the only image that's important to have stamped on your heart is the image of Jesus Christ. God is the ultimate source of value. All value comes from Him. And as we pursue Him, our very lives become wrapped up in His value. We actually begin to look like Him. Isn't that what John said?

Dear friends, now we are children of God, and what we will be has not yet been made known. But we know that when he appears, we shall be like him, for we shall see him as he is. (1 John 3:2, NIV)

And in the end, when it's all over, everything we work for in the name of Jesus bears fruit a hundredfold. Every treasure we earn in His service shines with undiminished beauty and awaits our possession. Every life we touch in His name causes a chain reaction of good reaching into eternity itself.

Why in the world should I waste my time chasing shadows, desert mirages, and house-of-mirrors reflections? Why should I serve other lords who aren't lords at all, care nothing for me, and never will?

There's only room for one lady's picture in my wallet. Her name is Joyce.

And there's only room for one Lord in my heart and yours. His name is Jesus.

WHY IS GOD JEALOUS?

Satan, the deceiver, has been in the image business for six thousand years, give or take.

He's had time and motivation to work hard at his craft and to refine his methods. He knows very well how powerful and intoxicating the images he weaves can be, and what devastating effect they can produce in human lives. He knows how false gods can turn men and women and boys and girls away from the true and living God who loves them to chase after shadows and empty illusions.

The truth is (if you wanted to make a study of it), that behind every idol, behind every false image, behind every counterfeit Christian cult, there is a demon—an agent of Satan to deceive, mislead, and eventually destroy its worshipers. (See 1 Corinthians 10:20–21.)

But the Lord is in the image business, too. And He is in business for the opposite reason. The desire of His heart is to raise men and women to a level of intimate fellowship with Himself.

At creation, God said, "Let Us make man in Our image, according to Our likeness" (Genesis 1:26). And through all the ups and downs, highs and lows, heartbreaks and delights of life on this earth, His one desire is to mold us—hour by hour, day by day—into the image of His Son, Jesus Christ. Scripture says, "For whom He foreknew, He also predestined to be conformed to the image of His Son" (Romans 8:29).

Through the shining, endless morning of eternity, those of us who have trusted Jesus Christ as Savior will bear His wonderful image. "And just as we have borne the likeness of the earthly man [Adam], so shall we bear the likeness of the man from heaven" (1 Corinthians 15:49, NIV).

God has very clear reasons for asking us to put Him first: In eternity we will reflect the glory of the Bright Morning Star, His precious Son. And here in our short, often troubled stay on earth, He knows that His love has the power to shape us and to deliver us.

In Romans 12, Paul warns: "Don't let the world around you squeeze you into its own mold, but let God remold your minds from within, so that you may prove in practice that the plan of God for you is good, meets all his demands and moves toward the goal of true maturity" (Romans 12:1–2, Phillips).

I know this: I want our children and our children's children—and their children after them until the Lord returns—to know that when we put God on the top of our list, He will put us on the top of His. God said that He would honor our lives and our children's lives as we obey and follow Him. But the opposite is also true, and ought to frighten us to contemplate: If we worship another "god" it will have a hurtful, damaging impact on generations to come. Your decision to either follow the Lord or chase false images will affect your loved ones—and children born into your family line for many years to come, should the Lord delay His coming.

Let's look again at the second commandment in its entirety:

"You shall not make for yourself a carved image—any likeness of anything that is in heaven above, or that is in the earth beneath, or that is in the water under the earth; you shall not bow down to them nor serve them. For I, the LORD your God, am a jealous God, *visiting the iniquity of the fathers on the children to the third and fourth generations of those who hate Me, but showing mercy to thousands, to those who love Me and keep My commandments."* (Exodus 20:4–6)

You can't miss the serious implications here. This passage says that the way you and I respond to this command will not simply affect us, it will mark the lives of those who follow after us—to the third and fourth generations! No, this doesn't mean that because of my sins, my kids and grandkids will be punished. The emphasis of Scripture is always on personal responsibility. No matter what your parents or grandparents may have been, you won't answer for their sins. *But for good or ill, you will be affected by their life decisions.*

If you live indifferently to the things of the Lord, if you continually give in to every suggestion of the flesh, if you have a love affair with materialism and acquiring things at any cost, if you chase after empty, hollow images for the rest of your life, the consequences for your children will be great. The simple fact is, none of us live unto ourselves; that is not the way God has wired His universe.

It's easy to see why God said, "Don't make any graven images." God knew that if we put the things of this world first, then everybody we love will be affected. But He gives the positive side of the coin, too. In verse 6 it says that if you humbly bow before Him and put Him first, then thousands of people will be affected by the righteousness in our lives—beyond the reach of our eyes or our expectations or even our imaginations.

Every one of us will leave an "image" of one kind or another after we are gone from this earth—in the sense that others will remember us in a particular way. What kind of image do you want it to be?

I was blessed with a model to follow in my life. I will never, never forget the image of my mother. She had very little of this world's goods. No fashion statement, for sure. She looked plain, but always very neat—and was dearly loved by everyone. She worked day and night, and whatever she had, she spent on her kids. Without a doubt, she was the sweetest, most wonderful person I've ever known.

What made her so attractive to everyone was the inner beauty of her life. She was convinced that you should make the *inside* of your life the priority. Mom always put God first. Period. The reason I'm in the pastorate and writing books like this one today is because my mom prayed for me every single day. I have no doubt that those prayers have had an immeasurable effect on my life.

What kind of image do you want to leave?

I'll let you in on a secret: Our boys aren't all that impressed that their dad pastors a large church, or knows a little Greek, or has written a few books. It's nice, and I'm sure they're happy about those things in their own way, but it is really no big deal. My walk with Jesus Christ, however, *is* a big deal. The reality of my love relationship with God overshadows *everything* else. I want to live a life before our boys that might give them hope. I want them to see a father who is real and has experienced the help of God regularly. I want them to see me praying. I want them to see me seeking God in my hurt and my perplexity and in my anxiety, as well as in the glad, good times. By God's grace, I want that image to be *burned in their minds* after I'm gone.

What are the elements in the image you will leave? They may include a Bible, well-worn from constant use and study. They may include an old chair in the living room where you prayed every morning. But I can tell you this: when you and I are gone, our kids won't talk about the toys we left. They won't care a whit about the newspaper clippings or the bowling trophies. What they will talk about and remember (if we've given them anything to remember at all), will be those things of eternal value.

Idols and false images rob the days of our lives from us and leave us with nothing. No peace. No satisfaction. No legacy for the ones we love. And what are idols, once again? *Idols are anything that take our focus off of God.*

Accept no substitutes! In Hong Kong, you can buy a watch that has the letters R-O-L-E-X written across the face. And it really looks like a Rolex. It's heavy like a Rolex. It gleams in the sunlight like a Rolex. But it's not a Rolex, and it will never perform like a Rolex. It's a cheap knockoff. You can buy counterfeits of name brands and real things all over the world. And all over the world, there are other gods who masquerade as the living God and seek your time, your life energies, and your allegiance. But when life begins to crumble beneath you like eroded sand under a beachfront condo, you will discover that these gods are not God and cannot help you. They will be as a curse to you.

In verse 5, God states that He is a jealous God.

Isn't that an odd statement? God? *Jealous?* But He makes no apology; He is very, very jealous for you and me. Yes, let's immediately agree that "jealousy" means something much different to God than it might mean to you or me. It's certainly not flavored by pettiness, narrowness, selfishness, or insecurity, as our "jealousy" might be.

Here's how I see it: My God knows me. *Of course He does.* He has known me from the womb. He has known me from before the foundations of the earth. He knows how I tick. He knows and wants what's best for me and those I love. And He doesn't want anything—no idol, no image, no false god, no phony divine knockoff—to stand in the way of my fulfillment.

God's jealousy suggests that He cares for us so much that He watches us all day long. He's greatly concerned about us. He knows how I'm living, where I go, and what I'm thinking moment by moment.

Frankly—back when I had a more narrow, negative view of God—that thought used to bother and worry me some. It almost seemed as though He were stalking me, and that I didn't dare take one false step. But I've learned that there's a reason why He always keeps His eye on me, and why He concerns Himself about my every decision. *He loves me.* He doesn't watch me because He's just waiting for me to make a mistake or catch me in some fault, but because He wants what's best for me.

When you stop to think about it, we really don't have a lot of years to throw away here on earth. We don't have endless time to dabble and experiment and play around. Our lives here are incredibly short—like a little puff of wind that bends the grass for a moment and then is gone. The psalmist prayed, "Remember how short my time is" (Psalm 89:47). And He does. He remembers. He knows. God knows us so well and knows how we can maximize the brief time we have on earth—how we can get the most out of life and avoid the false images and use-less pursuits that will sap our life and vitality.

A mother watches her child when he's at play, not because she is looking for ways to stifle him or ruin his life, but because she doesn't want him to run out in front of a car or to hurt him-self or to be carried away by a kidnapper or molester.

There are spiritual kidnappers and molesters loose in our world too. And they would capture us in our youth, take away our innocence, grind our hope into the dirt, hurt us very deeply, and cast us aside when we are ruined and broken. Just as the mother is jealous for her child's welfare, God is jealous for our welfare.

God watches us closely because He knows what is before us. He knows the issues of our lives better than we do. He understands the long-range implications of our every thought and every action. *If you loved as God loves and you saw as He sees, you would be concerned, too!* He sees our lives in total. He sees the day of our departure, and the future generations stretching out before us. He knows how one foolish, selfish decision can affect not only our lives, but the lives of our sons and daughters and their sons and daughters for *generations*. He sees how those I love could or potentially would be impacted by what I do or fail to do.

Because of these things, He is jealous when I flirt with destructive false images. He takes note as I begin to pursue my idols of choice and the glittery, seductive things of the world. God knows that down the road I'm going to be extremely sorry for the life I lived and the things I have pursued. He can see the end of every one of my actions, not only in my life, but in the lives of my sons and daughters and *their* sons and daughters on into eternity. It's as though our every action unleashes a string of dominoes that we can't stop. He who knows the end from the beginning is jealous for us that each action, thought, or decision will lead to life and joy and fruit and promise. To us, these decisions of life may seem arbitrary or casual; to the Eternal One, each decision is heavy with meaning and implication. That's why He commands us to walk carefully!

Live life, then, with a due sense of responsibility, not as men who do not know the meaning and purpose of life but as those who do. Make the best use of your time, despite all the difficulties of these days. Don't be vague, but firmly grasp what you know to be the will of the Lord. (Ephesians 5:15–17, Phillips)

In Psalm 23, we read that He wants to lead us in paths of righteousness. Why? Because He wants to take us away from better, more delightful paths? Because He wants to spoil our fun? No, but rather because He knows the very paths that will restore our souls!

How many people have you read about—or possibly even know—who have burned themselves out after pursuing worldly success or pleasure at any cost? And in the end, they find themselves so weary and worn out that they can't go on. They're pursuing an image, and it dances on ahead of them like the proverbial elusive butterfly, always just out of reach. So people hurry to be first. They hurry to be best. They hurry to succeed. They hurry to indulge in pleasure and "have fun." But it all becomes so wearisome. And in the end many say, "I just can't go on."

Ernest Hemingway was a man who appeared to have everything. A brilliant and gifted writer, he enjoyed a great measure of literary success and acclaim. Yet in 1961, in Ketchum, Idaho, he put a gun to his head and pulled the trigger. He just couldn't go on. Entertainers Elvis Presley, Janis Joplin, Jimi Hendrix, and John Belushi all became involved with drug addictions and just burned themselves out. They died young. They died too soon. They never found the green pastures or still waters. They never found the paths of righteousness that would restore and renew their weary souls.

They missed it! They missed *life*. But God is jealous that we enter into all that He has planned for us. God is jealous for us that we might experience rest and restoration in the deepest places of our soul.

While the world seeks to reshape us into a fickle, ever-changing image, the Lord tells us in Ephesians 4:24 to "put on the new self, which in the likeness of God has been created in righteousness and holiness of the truth" (NASB).

Oh, what a dear price we pay to clutch and cling to what the world offers. We see people selling their souls for things that God offers freely! He says in Matthew 6:33, "But seek first the kingdom of God and His righteousness, and all these things shall be added to you." The world says, "Seek influence, wealth, power, and pleasure." Yet God says, "Put Me first."

People say, "Well, I'll do what I want to do. My life is my life, I'm captain of my own soul, so I'll live it the way I want." It's true, you can live that way. You can make that choice. *But you don't get to choose the consequences of those choices.* Yes, you can certainly do what you want to do…but I'll tell you this: Had David known the consequences of his decision to have an affair with Bathsheba, he never would have gone through with it. Had David known how painful and expensive that choice would be, it wouldn't have been a hard decision to make. He would have left that rooftop, taken a cold shower, and gone back to bed, instead of doing what he did. As it was, he had to stand by and watch the utter devastation of his family and children through the years. It broke his heart. He wept many, many tears over that one quick, impulsive decision.

We are living in a generation that has thrown God to the wind and is committed to the very same idols spoken of in Scripture: gods who demand everything and give nothing. They say, "Worship me and you'll be happy. Wear my stuff and you'll be irresistible."

God says to us, "The reason I'm asking you not to place any object or enterprise or image ahead of Me is because I don't want you to wake up one day with a broken heart, as you watch your loved ones making the same mistakes you made, tripping over the same rocks you tripped over, and struggling with the same cynical attitudes that afflicted you…because your life will dramatically affect and influence them."

And when it does, you will watch with pain and disappointment and grief in your heart.

Just imagine for a moment that you are God. And you know that within yourself you have a fountain of the sweetest, purest, coolest, most refreshing water anyone could ever drink. And as you look down at a group of people you love very much, you see a deep, almost frantic thirst. But instead of coming to you for the water you would offer freely, they are trying to dig wells or cisterns for themselves to try to capture and hold water from an uncertain source. And their cisterns are so pitiful! From your vantage point in heaven, you can readily see that they are full of cracks and faults. As God, you know very well that these cisterns could *never* hold water. They will leave these people that you love thirstier and more desolate than ever. In fact, they will die in their thirst, when all they had to do was call out to you for all the cool, wonderful water they could ever drink.

How do you feel about that…if you are God?

Does it stir you a little?

Does it touch your heart?

Does it make you jealous for the time and energy and useless labor that these people are pouring into this hopeless project? Can't you imagine responding as the Lord actually did respond to the prophet Jeremiah?

"Be appalled, O heavens, at this,
and shudder, be very desolate," declares the LORD.
"For My people have committed two evils:
they have forsaken me,
the fountain of living waters,
to hew for themselves cisterns,
broken cisterns,
that can hold no water."
(Jeremiah 2:12–13, NASB)

How pained God must feel to think that He has offered living water—fresh every day—free for the taking. But you have chosen another way; you have chosen to dig your own cistern, because you're going to catch your own water and do it your own way. You're going to seek another option. But it's a *broken* option. It's a joke—it's no good. The very thing that you thought would keep you, sustain you, satisfy you, and fulfill you will be bone dry in the very hour when you need it most.

Sin is hard work. Digging a cistern out of solid rock is grievous toil. But in the end, it's never going to be what you thought it was going to be. It just won't hold water.

The old commentator Matthew Henry said it very well. Please read these words carefully.

When they came to quench their thirst there they found nothing but mud and mire, and the filthy sediments of a standing lake. Such idols were to their worshippers, and such a change did those experience who turned from God to them. If we make an idol of any creature—wealth, or pleasure, or honor—if we place our happiness in it, and promise ourselves the comfort and satisfaction in it which are to be had in God only, if we make it our joy and love, our hope and confidence, we shall find it a cistern, which we take a great deal of pains to hew out and fill, and at the best it will hold but a little water, and that dead and flat, and soon corrupting and becoming nauseous. Nay, it is a broken cistern, that cracks and cleaves in hot weather, so that the water is lost when we have most need of it. Let us therefore with purpose of heart cleave to the Lord only, for whither else shall we go? He has the words of eternal life.

God is jealous for you because He loves you.

Yet He has given you a free will, He will allow you to chase empty idols and false images for the rest of your life. He will allow you to dig your own cistern, to pick up a shovel and scrape away at the rocky soil through the days and weary years until your hands bleed and you are worn away by your useless toil. If you insist upon it, He'll let you have your own way.

But you'll have to walk right by His open arms to do it.

❦

Lord, I must admit that at times You seem to work rather slowly. There are times, in my anxiety and impatience, when I question Your wisdom, love, and purpose for my life. In the midst of prayers unanswered and difficulties unsolved, help me to remember that You are still in control! Forgive me for trying to take things into my own hands. Forgive me for turning to other solutions that are really no solutions at all. Forgive me for buying into the quick-fix theology so popular in the world today. Every other answer, every other "god" is a sad imitation that leaves me dissatisfied and unfulfilled. Lord, I refuse to allow the world to stamp its image on me.

And so today, Lord, let me never take You for granted or treat the holy things of God lightly. In Jesus' name, amen.

"You shall not take the name of the LORD your God in vain,
for the LORD will not hold him guiltless
who takes His name in vain."

EXODUS 20:7

꧁꧂

CHAPTER 4

TAKE CARE
WITH THE NAME

NAME EQUALS CHARACTER

What if you were to see your own mother's name in print on the next line? _____.

What thoughts would race through your mind in an instant? What images would leap to the screen of your memory? What emotions would brush across your heart?

When you hear a familiar name—any familiar name— thoughts and associations immediately surface in your mind, don't they? When people say "Jacqueline Kennedy," what do you think about? What do you see in your mind's eye? How about "Martin Luther King Jr." or "Ronald Reagan"? You could do the same with "Adolf Hitler" or "Winston Churchill" or "D. L. Moody" or "Michael Jordan." You think about certain things. You remember certain events. Perhaps you experience certain emotions. Why? Because those names *represent* something to you about certain individuals: who they are, what they've done, how they've lived. The names are a summary to you of all that those individuals are.

As a pastor, one of my favorite jobs is dedicating little children and their parents before God's people. It's a delight just to speak the names of the little ones aloud before the congregation. Some of the names come right out of the Bible…I've held Jonah, Micah, Joshua, and David in my arms. I've prayed over Rachel, Ruth, and Mary (no Dorcas yet, as of this writing). I've kissed Daniel, Esther, and Matthew on top of their downy little heads. I know of a number of people who actually make a prophetic decision to name their children a certain name because of what that name means to them. We certainly did with our boys, Ron Jr. and Mark. Ron's name simply means "strong one." Mark's means "mighty warrior." Their names have become typical and characteristic of them.

Ron is a young man of very strong convictions, who has not compromised, but has held to what he's known is really right. Those convictions served him well during his college years at Yale University. And Mark is one of those guys who's a real defender of the underdog, who stands up for anyone who needs help. He's one of those people who will take on any task and never shy away from entering into the fray. If there is something that needs to be done, he will step right up to it without any fear at all.

My wife Joyce's name means "joyful," which she certainly is. From day one, she's always been the light and joy of our home.

People's names represent something. A name represents who they are, and possibly (in a prophetic sense), who they might become. God was so concerned about this phenomenon that He actually named people Himself, or changed their names at certain key moments of their lives. When their character changed, He changed their name.

He told Abraham, "No longer shall your name be called Abram ["Exalted Father"], but your name shall be Abraham ["Father of a Multitude"]; for I have made you a father of many nations" (Genesis 17:5). The Lord Jesus changed Simon's name to Peter—a Rock. The Lord was telling Peter that he would be changed from a wishy-washy, unreliable man to someone who was firm and strong and would take a stand.

When a man or woman receives Jesus Christ as Savior, his or her name becomes *eternal;* it is written down in the Lamb's book of life. If a name represents a person's character and reputation, and is very important to God, why is there so much profanity today? Why do so many people casually take the name of our heavenly Father and our Lord Jesus in vain?

We can sense perhaps why this might be an issue of deep concern to the Lord. But why would He make it one of the Ten Commandments? Why such a stern warning? Why all the caution? Do you think it is possible that God knows something about what will happen to my life if I become careless and flippant about the name of God?

We live in a day, of course, where the air is blue with profanity. You can hardly watch a movie, pick up a novel, or even listen to the radio without hearing God's name taken in vain. One of the definitions for the word *profane* speaks of "debasing or defiling that which is holy or worthy of reverence." It's an attack against something holy. It's an attempt to take something exalted or revered and jerk it down from its pedestal. When I profane something, I try to yank it down to my level, so I can reduce it to being nothing more than I am.

What does it mean, then, to profane the Lord God? It is

nothing less than a denial of His holiness and majesty and power. It is an attempt to somehow pull God down to a common level and make Him equal with me.

And that is a grave and serious business.

There are those outside the Lord who can't stand to think of anyone or anything "higher" or "more lofty" than they are. On a greatly smaller scale, look what the tabloids and gossip magazines seek to do to "celebrities." The public seems to have an insatiable appetite for anything that would drag famous athletes or performers, presidents, princesses, preachers, and high officials down to the lowest level. When that happens we can say, "They're no better than me. I'm as good as they are."

And by cursing, we are destroying the concept of a lofty God above us. I have succeeded in my own mind of feeling that I can take this God, who appears to be holy, and reduce Him to someone just like me. To follow that track to its logical conclusion, there truly would be "nothing sacred" in the universe. Nothing at all.

If you're not in a monastery, you'll probably hear the word *damn* several times this week—or even before lunch today. What does that term mean? It means to condemn to a fate. People will seemingly damn anything and everything. It's G-D this, and G-D that. My G-D car, my G-D schedule, and my G-D back problems. It's so common. It seems to be part of common speech. Does it really matter?

Does *God* think it matters?

I'll tell you how much it matters—He made it one of the Ten Commandments. Why would He include it? *Because He knows that every time those terms are used, incredible destruction comes into my life and the lives of those I love.* When you don't put God first, when you don't honor His name, I'm going to tell you, life just doesn't work. It *does* matter when we use God's name in vain.

There may be more to God's order of things than many people think. I've heard men say, "G-D this home! G-D that woman! G-D those kids." I don't think they have any real idea of what they've just said. I don't think they have any concept that *these words and terms do not fall on deaf ears.* In the book of Matthew, Jesus warns us: "But I tell you that men will have to give account on the day of judgment for every careless word they have spoken" (Matthew 12:36, NIV). The Lord went on to say, "Your words now reflect your fate then: either you will be justified by them or you will be condemned" (12:37, TLB).

My friend Jack Hayford tells about an incident when he was on vacation years ago. The family was out driving in the country, and Jack pulled into a little two-pump gas station and general store to gas up. The attendant walked up to the pump, greasy hat askew and chewing on a toothpick. He greeted Jack warmly and began to fill the tank. As the man was doing so, he happened to look down at the tires on the Hayfords' car.

"You know," he told Jack, "I think you oughta know that your G-D tire is about to blow. If it does, you and your family will have a wreck. I think if I were you, I'd get a new tire."

Jack said, "Could you please take care of that?"

"Sure can," the man replied.

And while this man worked on the car, it seemed to Jack that every other word was G-D this and G-D that. This G-D car and these G-D tires and those G-D highways.

Finally Jack couldn't take any more. He looked at the man and said, "Sir, I don't *want* God to damn my car. I wish you wouldn't say that."

The man looked startled. "Oh," he said. "I'm sorry I offended you."

Jack said, "You know, sir, you work with tires, and you spared my family from an accident and possible disaster—and I'm grateful. But I'm a pastor. I work with souls. And when I heard you talking like that, I thought, *He spared my family from disaster; I want to spare him from disaster.* So you need to hear me when I say that using God's name in vain is a very, very expensive thing to do. You can't use the Lord's name in vain and not pay a price."

Why would God say, "Don't take My name in vain"? Because He loves you and me so much. The problem with most people is that they think they can get by with it because they say anything they want to and "nothing has happened." Yet when you read the Scriptures you discover something about sowing and reaping, and it is this: You never, never reap in the same season you sow. But God's Word is true. *And using His name in vain will affect your life.*

When we use the name of God in a careless way, when we readily call upon Him to "damn" or condemn a person or place or situation, it is my belief that we set something in motion in the spirit—something beyond our finite understanding.

There is power in the name of our God. There is power in the name of Jesus Christ. Do you believe that? Do you believe that demons screamed and writhed and tore themselves from their hosts at the mention of His name? Do you believe that in the authority of His voice, and the authority of His name, that the eyes of the blind were opened, that withered legs were made strong, and that dead bodies came up out of the grave?

So why wouldn't we believe there are consequences to the way we use His name? Good consequences for using it rightly, evil consequences for using it casually or with evil intent. There are consequences to the name of God whenever it's used.

What are we saying when we say G-D to someone? Are we "damning" something in them? Are we knocking something down, are we pressing something back in them when we say that? If to damn means to "consign to a fate," aren't we saying, "May you come to destruction! May you have a destructive end!"

Please remember God gave us this third command because He loves us. He's not just saying, "Hey, I'm really somebody and I'd like you to start reverencing My name, if you don't mind." Certainly His name is important to Him, but God loves you and me, and when you love someone, what do you do? You constantly remind them of the consequences to their actions.

And in this case, there is not only a consequence, there is ultimately disaster.

When I hear people casually use those terms, they have no idea the *damning results* of the words they use. There is incredible power in the words that are spoken in the lives of people like you and me. We reverence His name because there is power in that name. God knows that the words I speak will tend to affect what I actually experience in life. There is a correlation! Oh, the need to reverence His name.

What did David say? "For You, O God, have heard my vows; You have given me the heritage of those who fear Your name"

(Psalm 61:5). David is saying, for all those who fear His name, love His name, and honor His name, that the Lord brings those people into a heritage—the heritage of those who have honored His name down through the years since time began. It is a heritage of blessing and honor. It is a heritage of fruitfulness and life impact and great joy.

How could we not honor Him? How could we dishonor the very source of all honor and blessing? For that matter…how could we stand by silently while His name is being dragged through the mud? How could we go on watching a movie or reading a book where the name of Jesus is deliberately defamed? I have seen men beat up men because of something somebody said about a wife, a girlfriend, a mother, or a sister. I've seen men ready to risk life and limb to defend the name and reputation of a loved one. Names are important! And certainly the name of God, the Name above every name, is important.

Why in the world would God say, "I want My name to be precious to you"? Why would He make such a point of never using that name in a casual way?

Think of this: There is eternal salvation in the name. His name means life. In John 20:31, Scripture says: "But these [things] are written that you may believe that Jesus is the Christ, the Son of God, and that believing you may have life in His name.

Acts 4:12 reinforces that:

"Nor is there salvation in any other, for there is no other name under heaven given among men by which we must be saved."

There is no other name. Salvation from eternal hell is found in no other name. And that is the name we would casually misuse or deliberately drag through the mud?

Picture in your mind a horrible darkness, filled with despair and agony and fear and loneliness and death. Then picture an open door...a door that opens into life and hope and beauty and healing and boundless joy. Can you imagine someone spitting on that door or throwing filth on it? Can you conceive of someone taking a spray can and scribbling over it with vile graffiti? Jesus is that door! The very doorway into life. The world's only hope. The only escape from hell and eternal despair. There is no other door! And this is the door we would treat with casual contempt?

People may say, "Well, I just grew up around this kind of talk," or "I just learned to talk this way because I've been around the boys." We try to say that what comes out of our mouths is really no indication of what we have in our hearts. *Yet Scripture always links what comes out of our mouths with our hearts.*

Jesus Himself said this again and again. It was important enough to *Him* to repeat.

- ♦ "You brood of vipers, how can you who are evil say anything good? For out of the overflow of the heart the mouth speaks." (Matthew 12: 34, NIV)
- ♦ "But the things that come out of the mouth come from the heart, and these make a man 'unclean.'" (Matthew 15:18, NIV)
- ♦ "The good man brings good things out of the good stored up in his heart, and the evil man brings evil things

out of the evil stored up in his heart. For out of the overflow of his heart his mouth speaks." (Luke 6:45, NIV)

Admit it or not, like it or not, the mouth speaks what is in
the heart. The way you talk is because of the way your heart is,
and the Lord knows that. You cannot say, "Well, she has a vile
mouth but a good heart." You cannot say, "Well, he's got a problem with bad language, but he really does have a heart of gold."

No, she doesn't!

No, he doesn't!

I'm sorry, but according to the Lord's own words, that cannot be. The Bible says that the way an individual speaks is an
accurate barometer of his or her heart.

James wrote: "But no man can tame the tongue. It is an
unruly evil, full of deadly poison. With it we bless our God and
Father, and with it we curse men, who have been made in the
similitude of God. Out of the same mouth proceed blessing and
cursing. My brethren, these things ought not to be so. Does a
spring send forth fresh water and bitter from the same opening?
Can a fig tree, my brethren, bear olives, or a grapevine bear figs?
Thus no spring can yield both salt water and fresh" (James
3:8–12).

The bitter, hurtful, or profane words that come out of my
mouth are a sign to me that something is terribly wrong in my
heart. Have you ever heard yourself making a statement that
comes out sounding so bitter you are almost surprised by it? It
sounded so acidic that you immediately try to soften it. You say,
"Well, I didn't mean that quite the way it sounded." But what
you really mean is that you didn't mean to say it *out loud* quite

the way you did. But in your heart, you really are that bitter. And what comes through your mouth is an overflow of that.

When I say something profane or crude or bitter, it ought to immediately prompt me that something is wrong with my heart. It ought to be a kind of wake-up call. I ought to get alone with the Lord as quickly as I can and ask the Holy Spirit to search and examine my heart.

Is God concerned with what you say? Yes. Because He knows that there is something greater than what's wrong with your mouth. It's your heart. He knows that it is out of the overflow of the heart that the mouth speaks. It's a reminder to me that swearing speaks of disorder and turmoil in the heart. And people who talk like this have no idea of its lethal power. You find an angry and profane person and I'll show you one whose life is out of order. It's very typical. They go hand in hand. God knows how much using His name in vain is going to affect you and me.

Perhaps you say, "Well, I don't do that. I don't talk that way. I don't swear. I would never say G-D anything. I'm a Christian, and I would never talk that way."

But there are other ways to use His name in vain—socially acceptable ways to profane Him. I have been guilty of them in my life, and perhaps you have, too. And one of those ways is to be very, very casual or careless in our prayers. The Lord cautions us against "vain repetitions." *Vain* means empty. It means saying things over and over, without conviction.

There are those who would twist Scripture and say, "Now, when you come to the Lord, just ask Him for whatever you want. A bigger house, a new car, a better job, new clothes. Then when you're done, just say, 'in Jesus' name, amen,' and you'll get whatever you ask for."

Does Scripture say such a thing? Is the Lord pleased when we use His name in such a "prayer"?

Why *do* we say "In Jesus' name" at the end of our prayers? Is it like, "I'm signing off…over and out"? "In Jesus' name…I'll catch ya tomorrow." Why do we say those words? Here's why. Because when we pray, we're saying that everything that we just asked for, we believe in our hearts is the very thing that Jesus would be asking for if He were doing the asking. Knowing this should alter the way we pray. We will be more careful about making a list of selfish demands and ending the prayer by muttering, "In Jesus' name." Before I use His name, I need to first ask myself, "Is this what He would be asking for? Is this what He wants?"

A recent poll concluded that 60 percent of Americans say they have used God's name in vain. I think the number would be more like 100 percent. All of us have done it. There have been times when we have uttered His name in prayer, but it was a selfish prayer. And if we had really analyzed it, we would have doubts as to whether this was what God really wanted for us, or even if that was really what we truly wanted. There is something in my own heart that I've wanted. There's something I've desired and wanted, but never checked to see if that's what the Savior would really want me to be asking for.

Vain means empty. It certainly applies to asking for things in Jesus' name with no sense of conviction that this is what He truly wants.

Also…many of us believers become so "at home" with the

name of our Lord and Savior that we feel we can use it in a cute or jesting way, because "after all, we're part of the family." Someone, for instance, will comment on a planned vacation to Hawaii, and we'll say, "Oh yes, you'll just be suffering for Jesus." Is that an empty use of His noble name? Vain means empty, and that's what such a comment really is. It's something that we don't mean. It's something we've said for a clever quip or a quick laugh, and we've dragged the name of our Lord into it.

Are we really, really careful? This is the name to which every knee shall bow. This is the name that carries with it power when it is spoken. There is life and salvation in this name. Do we get too cozy with this name? Too familiar? In the Lord's prayer, Jesus said, "When you pray, say, 'Hallowed be Your name.'" *When you acknowledge the holiness of God, it is impossible to be casual!* When you come to see Him for who He is and what He has done, there is no way in the world you could ever treat Him casually again, and you couldn't treat His name casually. Why? Because you acknowledge the great price that He paid and the great work that He's done.

Once you have a vision of God, you'll have a vision of yourself. When you see Him, you'll see you!

What was Isaiah's first response when He saw the Lord in all His holiness and might? "Oh no, I'm doomed because of my mouth! I've said unclean, unworthy things!"

Another thought. Can you ever imagine an angel, who stands in the presence of God, taking His name casually? A thousand times no! We can learn from the angels how to honor the name of God.

How should I respond, then? I suggest three simple steps.

1. *Recognize Sin and Confess It.*

Confession means "to speak the same as." It means, Lord, I agree with You. Tell Him you're sorry you used His name in vain, because if You do, He will wash your heart clean. Did you ever have your mom wash your mouth out with soap? That's only a momentary deterrent. What we need is to have our hearts washed. Which brings us to the second thing:

2. *Accept His Forgiveness.*

Just tell Him, "Lord I agree with You. No wonder, Lord, there is so much disarray and confusion in my life, my home, and my business. I have not honored Your name. I have not entered into the heritage of those who fear Your name. I have not honored You as the Lord and the love of my life. Accepting His forgiveness means remembering that *all* of our sins were placed on the shoulders of the Lord Jesus on the cross. He paid for every one of them. He suffered the wrath of God for every time we have profaned God's name or used it in a casual, careless way. He paid the price for our sins and offers forgiveness and reconciliation to us.

3. *Practice God's Presence.*

Remember, He's always there. He hears everything, sees everything, knows everything. If I used God's name in vain, and my boys heard me, I know that I would be setting something in motion in their lives that will affect them later on—perhaps the potential to begin to be casual about the things of God. Practicing God's presence affects your speech, because you know He's ever-present. He's listening to my every word and my every prayer.

One of the things I love about the Lord is that, while all of us have made mistakes, all of us have run in the wrong direction, and all of us have said things we wished we hadn't said, God says, "If you'll come to Me, then I'll wash you clean. I'll erase all of those things in your past, and I'll give you hope and joy for tomorrow."

If the Lord made this a commandment, I have no doubt in my mind that the reason He does this is because He loves us so much. Reading this commandment in light of His love for us gives us hope for tomorrow.

You say, "Well, Ron, I know I've used His name in vain and know in my heart that it was wrong. What can I do about it now?" Let me direct you for a moment to Psalm 130. Even though Scripture tells us that God keeps track of every idle word we speak in our lives, this psalm reassures us that there is forgiveness with this God!

David writes:

If You, LORD, should mark iniquities,
O Lord, who could stand?
But there is forgiveness with You,
That You may be feared.
(Psalm 130:3–4)

If He should hold the list of our iniquities against us, if He should hold the list of every time we have ever used His name casually or dishonorably, what hope would there be for any of us? But He has made provision for forgiveness, so that we can change our minds, change our hearts, change our direction, and begin to love and serve and fear this wonderful God.

Lord, I don't know why it has taken me so long to realize how blind I am. I now know that taking Your name in vain is as much an issue of the heart as it is the lips. Help me, O Searcher of hearts, to remember that it is out of the heart that the mouth speaks. Cleanse me, I pray, from the inside out. And Lord, please put a guard over my mouth, that I may never take You for granted or speak of You in a light or foolish way. I don't want to offer glib prayer and empty worship. Remind me often, Lord, that the place of fellowship with You, the place with green pastures and still waters, lies between Mt. Sinai and Mt. Calvary.

And so today, Lord, open my eyes to the fire and beauty of Your awesome holiness. Touch my lips and I will be clean. In Jesus' name, amen.

"Remember the Sabbath day, to keep it holy.
Six days you shall labor and do all your work,
but the seventh day is the Sabbath of the LORD your God.
In it you shall do no work....
For in six days the LORD made the heavens and the earth,
the sea, and all that is in them, and rested the seventh day.
Therefore the LORD blessed the Sabbath day and hallowed it."

EXODUS 20:8–11

CHAPTER 5

A TIME TO REFLECT

I woke up in the ICU to see a familiar face swim slowly into focus.

It was my dear friend Jack Hayford, and even in my medicated state I knew that expression on his face. Jack loves me very much, but I had a hunch he hadn't flown up from Los Angeles to quote poetry to me. And I was right.

"Good enough for you?" he asked.

What kind of greeting was that for a man in the ICU? What a strange thing to say to a friend hanging on to life after a near-fatal heart attack. But Jack was just getting warmed up.

"You're a prideful man, Ron," he told me. "You think people are really impressed that you work seven days a week."

I groaned. He'd said much the same thing to me many times before, but I'd always escaped by running to another appointment, taking a phone call, or changing the subject. Now I was stuck in a hospital bed, shackled by tubes and IVs and monitors, and I wasn't going anywhere. I could pretend to fall asleep, but I had a feeling Jack wouldn't buy it.

This time, he had me.

"This is an ego thing for you, isn't it, Ron? You want affirmation. You want everybody to say, 'Isn't he amazing? Look at that Ron Mehl. Always in the office. Never misses a service. Works seven days a week!' Get serious, Mehl. Whom are you trying to impress? *God?* Well, I can tell you something. He's not impressed. God's only impressed with one thing, and that's His Son."

As one of my closest friends for many years, Jack has certainly earned the right to speak to me that way. What's more, I knew that he was right, and that his words for me were as words from the Lord.

I *knew* that I violated one of God's life principles, and that I was paying the price.

There's no use denying it; I've struggled with this fourth command. To begin with, I've had trouble understanding why this Sabbath thing should even be one of "The Ten." Think about it. The Lord is going to give ten extremely important instructions—so important to His heart and to the life of His people that He will literally write them in stone with His finger, and hand-deliver them on a mountaintop. And with all the crucial, critical things in the world He might have said, He makes "remember the Sabbath day" number four?

Why?

If I had been doing it—if these were Mehl's ten commandments—it probably would have been number 47. Or maybe 202. Sure it's important. But alongside murder and adultery and coveting your neighbor's wife? Come on! Why in the world would the Lord make a law emphasizing rest and a special day?

Why does the Lord say a Sabbath rest is so important to us as His people?

Candidly, there is another reason why I struggle with this particular commandment. I feel a great and burning sense of urgency in my life these days. After my serious heart attack, an ongoing battle with leukemia, and the loss of several near and dear friends to death, I find it difficult *not* to think about work. I know that life is fragile, that time is short and that—well, there is so much to do. (Besides, I'm a pastor. So it's *God's* work, isn't it?)

So why does He give this particular command in His love? Why did He write it down in His "Father Knows Best" book for you and for me? What is it all about?

Through the years, it's never been difficult for me to see God's love at work in the circumstances of my life—even in the hard things. And I know very well that when I resist His principles, He disciplines me as the loving Father that He is. Through my long pastoral ministry, I have resisted this fourth commandment…and I have paid for that resistance.

In fact, I have paid very dearly.

No, I'm not saying that everybody who ignores the Sabbath will get sick or have a heart attack or wake up to find Jack Hayford in his face. But I am saying that if you consistently dishonor the Sabbath principle in your life, somewhere along the line the bills will come due. Things will begin to break down in your life. The breakdown may be physical, emotional, spiritual, financial, or marital. I can't tell you what form His discipline will take; but I know that God loves us too much to allow our self-destructive tendencies to go unchallenged.

Other people besides Jack had warned me strongly about this issue before the heart attack. Friends inside the church and outside the church were saying to me, "Ron, you'd better slow down. You'd better be careful!"

I had a nagging sense of conviction about it, too. I knew that the Lord was in those warnings. I knew in my heart I should be carving time out of the dawn-to-dark work schedule—more time to be with the Lord, more time to be with Joyce, more time to be with the boys, more time to rest my body and mind. But I just didn't do it. I didn't respond. I put it off.

I've pastored the same church for twenty-five years. It's my life. I love the Lord's people. I love my responsibilities. I love being a shepherd. And through the years, for countless weeks at a time, I have been at the church seven days a week. Not five. Not six. But every day.

But the heart attack—and a couple of other bone-jarring bumps in the road—was a very stern reprimand from God. I had violated His Sabbath principle for my life. He was telling me, "I love you, son, but this is not an option. These are not the Ten Suggestions."

But there are so many needs! So much hurt. So much opportunity. So many open doors. And somehow I keep wrestling with the idea that God "needs" more and more of me to get His work done. But the truth is, *I need more and more of Him.* As the church continues to grow, and the condition of families becomes more desperate, and the demands of the ministry go through the roof, I need more of His peace, more of His joy, more of His tenderness, more of His tough love, more of His wisdom, more of His resurrection life flowing through me. And the simple fact is He isn't going to give it to me in one-minute bursts between services or counseling appointments.

He wants time with me.

He wants to walk with me.

He wants to share His heart with me.

He wants a relationship.

During my days of recuperation, I sensed the Lord saying to me, "Son, if you continue to run from Me on this matter, these things won't be over soon. There will be more breakdowns, because I didn't build you to work seven days a week. And by the way, *I didn't work seven days either!* If you think you can live your life without taking that time to let Me renew and restore you, you are mistaken—and I am not pleased! What I said to My disciples I say to you, 'Come with Me by yourself to a quiet place and get some rest.'" (See Mark 6:31.)

Remember what David sang about the Lord?

The LORD is my shepherd;
I shall not want.
He makes me to lie down in green pastures;
He leads me beside the still waters.
He restores my soul....
(Psalm 23:1–3)

He *makes* me lie down! If you don't lie down and rest, if you don't seek out those quiet pastures and still waters with your Shepherd, it's not beyond Him to make you. You say, "Well, I don't believe God would do that." Then you don't know God! You don't understand His Father love! If you're not going to slow down and rest, then look around at the circumstances of your life and find out why you're in the condition you're in. Maybe He loves you more than you think.

Please note that the phrase "He makes me lie down" comes *before* the words "He restores my soul." It is as we enter into His rest that we experience His wonderful healing touch on our lives. Restoration is neither quick nor cheap.

By the way, Jack Hayford didn't leave my bedside that day with those hard words still floating in the air. He sat down close beside me and put his hand on mine, and there were tears in his eyes. "Ron," he said gently, "I believe God is telling you that if you will honor the Sabbath principle in your life, God will fulfill the mighty plan He's purposed for you." And then he said, "You will live to see your grandchildren grow up."

Our Lord gave these principles to us in love, for our protection. The first three commandments concern our relationship with this God who loves us. We should put Him first. We should never allow anything in between that relationship with Him. We should never put other gods before Him, or turn to "other options." He must be first! We must be careful to never dishonor His name, but rather to speak tenderly and truthfully of Him, as He speaks of us.

And the Sabbath? Maybe the Lord wants us to use this interval of rest (whether it's a day, two days, or half a day) to accomplish several things. Perhaps this break from the pressures of the week is a time to just sit down, be quiet, and while no one is around, ask yourself some questions: *Lord, are You really first in my life? Lord, is there anything between You and me? When I'm in trouble, facing hardships and difficulties, do I turn to You? When I'm lonely and bored and feeling empty, are You the one I seek? Lord, could it be that I've created some other gods and images that somehow satisfy me and fulfill my needs? Have I dishonored Your name this week, or spoken lightly of You? Do I love You less today than I did a week ago—or a year ago? Search my heart, O Lord!*

No matter where we are in life, giving ourselves over to workaholism or nonstop activities can be a great temptation. Overwork is celebrated by some and demanded by others. If you own your own company, you've made a great investment, so you feel the need to press the limits of physical and emotional strength to protect your investment.

But God has made a great investment in us, too. What was it old Peter said?

> For you know that it was not with perishable things such as silver or gold that you were redeemed from the empty way of life handed down to you from your forefathers, but with the precious blood of Christ. (1 Peter 1:18–19, NIV)

I wonder if the Sabbath isn't the day when you and I get to stop and remind ourselves…

of who God is,
of the terrible price He paid to buy us back from Satan's
   kingdom,
of what He has promised to do in us and through us,
of what He wants to accomplish in our hearts and lives,
   and

of the place He is preparing for us, when all our frantic scurrying across the face of this tiny planet will only be the dimmest of memories…and we will be caught up in Him alone.

A TIME FOR REST

My wife Joyce recently enlightened me with the news that if you bought a new pair of shoes today and wore them every day, they would wear out in about six months.

That particular thought had never occurred to me before, but I suppose that women (with immediate access to both sides of their brain) are able to keep track of such things. Joyce, of course, is always trying to convince me that when it's time to buy new shoes, she needs *two* pairs. (Can you imagine?) One of her theories is that if you have two pairs of shoes and alternate those shoes every other day, both pairs will last about two years. What's the difference if I wear them every day or alternate them? The leather or fabric (so she tells me) has a little bit of a rest, and it lasts significantly longer.

I might have been inclined to doubt her hypothesis if it wasn't for something I learned twenty-four years ago when we first arrived in Beaverton, Oregon, to pastor this congregation. At that time, there was a bowling alley a few blocks away from our little church building. And as I visited with one of the guys who worked there, I learned something amazing. It seems that every couple of weeks, this particular bowling establishment removed all of their bowling pins from service and put them on a shelf, alternating them with another full set of bowling pins out of storage. And do you know why they did this?

So that the bowling pins could rest.

"Come on," I told my new friend, "you're just pulling a preacher's leg. Bowling pins need to *rest?*"

He swore it was true. They apparently discovered that if the wooden pins don't "rest," they lose their vitality, and won't bounce around as much or be as "alive." All of that flipping and knocking around works a hardship on the pins, it seems, and eventually takes its toll. But if you give them a week off and set them in a corner, they'll come back stronger with more life than ever.

So...shoes need to rest and bowling pins need to rest. How do you top that? Well, my friends in agriculture tell me that even *dirt* needs to rest. If you have any farming in your background, you will know that farmers don't plant the same things in the same fields year after year. They may plant corn one year, but the next year they'll plant beans on the same parcel of ground. Why? Because the corn will take certain nutrients out of the soil, and the beans will put 'em back in. If a farmer can afford it, he will let whole tracts of ground lie fallow for a year or more, and not plant anything. Why? Because the land benefits from the rest. After a year or two of lying easy under wind and rain, snow and sun, it yields a greater, more bountiful crop.

Imagine that! Exodus 20:11 says that in six days the Lord made the heaven and earth, the sea, and all that is in them, and rested on the seventh day. Do you think the Lord might have some insights into His own creation? Do you think He might know something about you and me that we tend to forget? The

Lord knows us so well, doesn't He? And in His deep love for us, He knows how much we need to rest. To lie down. To reflect. To reconnect with Him, the very Author of life. He has built this need within us as surely as our need for water and food and oxygen.

David wrote, "O Lord, you have examined my heart and know everything about me. You know when I sit or stand.... You chart the path ahead of me, and tell me where to stop and rest" (Psalm 139:1–3, TLB).

Isn't that tender? He shows me where to stop and rest! But what if I brush right on by Him and refuse to stop? What if I think I know better, and that I really don't need to rest at all? That would be pretty foolish, wouldn't it? After all, if *God* took a day of rest, and all creation needs to rest (even bowling pins), then maybe you and I do, too. I think God is saying here, "You know something? I am extremely busy up here. I'm working all over the world—over countless worlds—keeping things in order, and holding things in place. I'm a busy person, and have lots to do, and you're a busy person and you have lots to do, too. But would it be possible that maybe, let's say one day a week, we could just make sure we set aside some time because of our love for one another? Is that too much to ask? Yes, we'll talk every day, hopefully. There will be times of worship, prayer, and daily devotion…but could we at least have one day where we could just talk and concentrate on one another and be with one another?"

I think that's what God had in His great heart with this fourth commandment. *Could we just have some time together?* God knows that if we get so busy and ahead of ourselves that we don't have time for Him, we'll simply wear out and wear down. David, as usual, says it so well:

> Just as a father has compassion on his children,
> so the LORD has compassion on those who fear Him.
> For He himself knows our frame;
> He is mindful that we are but dust.
> (Psalm 103:13–14, NASB).

We're made out of dust, and, as we noted earlier, even dirt needs to rest!

We are always the losers when we try to run ahead of God, striving to maintain a faster pace than He desires. Picture an impatient football running back who continually runs ahead of his blockers, getting battered and bruised and flattened. The first couple of times he does it—gaining an extra foot or two at great expense to his body—we marvel at his eagerness. But after three or four quarters of such play, we marvel at his ignorance! It's obvious Mr. Eager will burn out early in his career with multiple concussions and injuries and will never achieve his potential. He will be no further help to his team.

Scripture says so often to us, "Won't you just wait on the Lord?" Don't try to go faster than He intends. Find His pace and keep up with Him—neither running ahead nor lagging behind. When you do, you'll enjoy His close fellowship every step of the way.

There is a story I like very much about a wealthy American entrepreneur who went on a hunting safari in Africa. He chose a seasoned guide and hired local natives to carry the necessary gear. Aggressive and driven, the business mogul wanted to go much faster than his guide from the very first day. And every day after that, he pushed and drove his bewildered safari team from morning to night, until they could hardly stand.

Finally the burden bearers could go no farther; they would not stir from where they sullenly reclined in the shade. The American tycoon, used to instant obedience, was furious. "Get up, you bums!" he yelled. "Push on!" But they all just sat there, not even meeting his eyes. The impatient man stormed at his guide, "What's happening here? Why won't they go on?" The guide replied, "They must stay here all day. They won't move, no matter how much you shout and bully. We have been going too hard and fast, and *we must let our souls catch up with our bodies.*"

Some of us run ahead of God, even while trying to accomplish His purposes. Some of us (no names mentioned here!) have pushed on and on after God says, "Rest." That's why Joyce can sometimes wave her hand in front of my eyes and say, "Hello-o…are you in there? Anybody home?"

That's why people can be physically, bodily in church but "checked out" mentally, emotionally, and spiritually. That's why people can be with their kids in some activity, but not really "there" at all. If we make the Lord our priority, abide in Him, and walk in step with Him, He'll help our hearts to catch up.

A couple of words here from the apostle Paul throw even more light on this thought. As he was wrapping up his letter to the Romans, he wrote: "I know that when I come to you, I will come in the full measure of the blessing of Christ" (Romans 15:29, NIV). Isn't that great? Here was a man whose heart had caught up with his body. He knew that he was so connected with Christ, so full of Christ, that when he visited he would bring a FULL MEASURE of Christ's blessing into their lives.

How could he make such a claim? Maybe the biggest clue is in Galatians 5:25: He says, "If we live in the Spirit, let us also walk in the Spirit." The NIV renders it like this: "Since we live by the Spirit, *let us keep in step with the Spirit."*

I like that! Since we live by the Spirit, we might as well keep in step with Him. We might as well stay close to Him. We might as well walk at His pace. We might as well carry on a conversation with Him all day long and enjoy His companionship.

He knows the exact "pace" we ought to be walking through the days and years. He knows when we're running too fast, or hanging back too long. And as our Guide through life, He has things to show us that we may very well miss if we keep running ahead of Him in our foolish impatience.

Most of the world, of course, has dropped any pretense of honoring a special time with God. We have no time with God and no time for God. As far as our world is concerned, He is irrelevant. Remember in the early seventies when stores first began staying open on Sundays? Most of them started the practice by opening from 1 to 5 P.M., making at least a gesture toward customers and employees who might value being in church. Even that small courtesy, however, quickly went out the window as cash registers across America rang in fresh income. Sunday, in much of our nation, has become "just another day." I am told that here in the Portland area there isn't a soccer field in the city that isn't filled with kids' soccer teams playing soccer by 9:00 A.M. Sunday morning.

Church? *How irrelevant!* Worship? *What's that?*

Please don't miss my point here. Since we live in the New Testament era, I'm not pushing some kind of uptight, legalistic, sunrise-to-sunset "day of rest." Frankly, *every* day is a Sabbath day of rest for the believer in Jesus Christ. He *is* our Sabbath rest. And yet…even the principle of "one day for God," honored by our nation since colonial days, has been completely trampled in the dust by today's pleasure-mad, material-obsessed culture.

We have so little time left for God. Our lives are so very full, and yet so very empty. We have no room for Him in our thoughts, in our schedules, or in the fabric of our lives. The question is then, "What in the world do I do about it? Do I keep going along with the flow of the world and let them continually erode away my personal times of relationship with the Lord?

Solomon, wise man that he was, learned something very interesting about the way life works in God's world. He wrote: "Unless the LORD builds a house, the work of the builders is useless. Unless the LORD protects a city, guarding it with sentries will do no good. It is useless for you to work so hard from early morning until late at night, anxiously working for food to eat; for God gives rest to his loved ones" (Psalm 127:1–2, NLT).

In His love, I believe the Lord is saying this: "You work night and day. When you're not working, you're playing so hard you exhaust yourself. You're busy, busy, busy, with no time for God, no time to evaluate your heart and life. You think that by running at that pace, you'll get ahead. You think that if you don't cram every excess hour with work or entertainment, that you will somehow miss out on life and be the loser." But the Sabbath principle is the exact opposite! The fact is, time set aside for the Lord is never lost time. God knows what a great impact time alone with Him will make in our lives. He tells us, "When you stop working, I'll do My greatest work."

I can still remember being a starry-eyed high school kid, standing on the basketball court at Williams Arena on the campus of the University of Minnesota. We were playing a district championship game, and oh, how big I felt playing in that fabled arena. On that floor, it seemed like we could do anything. We could play over our heads. We could soar. We could defy gravity. I wanted to stay there forever. I didn't want the experience to end.

I also remember visiting the Garden Tomb on my first trip to Israel. It was such a peaceful place and time for me that I never wanted to leave. I wanted the tour to go on without me. Reflecting on those two significant moments in my life, it strikes me that God knows something about those quiet times alone with Him. I've never forgotten my time of standing on the Williams Arena floor or sitting in a quiet, restful place at the Garden Tomb because those times so impacted my life. I think God must want us to realize that "Sabbath" times with Him will do far more than that. He wants us to realize that those times in His presence—whether they occur on Saturday, Sunday, or Tuesday afternoon—are not wasted. In a sense, when you are with the Eternal One, time stands still. You see things in a new light, from a new perspective. You suddenly understand things about your activities and your priorities and your relationships that you had not understood before. He wants us to realize that those times are strategic investments...in both time and eternity.

What is so wonderful about this time of rest is the assurance that almighty God—my Creator and Redeemer, my Lord and my Friend—is working on my behalf to bring things about in my life. It isn't me. It isn't my work. It isn't my cleverness or energy or determination or luck or timing. It is *all* of Him.

I just get to rest.

A TIME FOR INVENTORY

My friend Dick Scott undertook the project of translating the Bible from English to the language of the Choco Indians of Panama. Well into the work, Dick and his assistant, Ricardo, ran into a frustrating snag.

They couldn't come up with a word for *praise*.

This was a very primitive tribe with no written language or alphabet. Yet the verbal constructions were so intricate that simply trying to conjugate a verb was sometimes mind-boggling.

Even so, the tribe didn't seem to have a term for praise. There was none.

Dick and Ricardo said, "What are we going to do here?" As they began talking to men and women around the village, the solution suddenly leaped out at them—as it so often does in translation work—in a casual conversation over a simple meal.

And what was that solution?

"It is good."

That was what the Chocos always said as they expressed pleasure. If somebody brought you a big bowl of soup or rice with a cooked snake in it, you would say, "Oh, this is *good!*" (Maybe you would say that, but I don't think I would!) And when these people said "This is good," what they meant was,

"This is *really* good. This is probably the best I've ever had!"

When God created the world and all that is in it, Scripture says that He worked for six days, looked back over what He had done, and said, "It is good." And we all know that His creation was not just "good," it was very, very good.

Can you and I say the same thing? When we look back at what we've done on some long-term project, can we say, "It is good"? When we reflect on all we've accomplished in a day, a week, a year, or a lifetime, can we say, "It is good"?

If you can't—if you can't reflect on your life, your home, your family, your labors, and speak those three words, maybe the reason is because *you* have done it. It's been *your* work, not God's. It's been *your* agenda. It's been *your* game plan. You have lived life on your own terms.

But when you know that you've taken your life, your home, your ministry, your work, your investments, and everything you are, and have placed it all in His care and rested it in His hand, you can have a different outlook. You can look back at the things you've done in His strength and with His help and say, "Lord, this is good. No one in the world may think much of this or even give it a second thought. I've never had my name in the newspaper or my face on TV and there haven't been a lot of people shaking my hand or slapping me on the back. But Lord, because Your hand and touch have been upon my life, *it is good.*"

I believe God intended the Sabbath as a day to consider such things…the very stuff of life itself. God intended that we spend quiet time with Him and ask questions such as these: "Are all these things I'm involved in 'good' in Your sight, Lord? Are they the best I could do with what You've given me? Am I doing these things in my own strength, Lord, or are You truly with me? Am I hearing Your voice? Am I following Your lead? Am I leaning on Your wisdom? Are these the sorts of things that will be burned up as wood, hay, and stubble in Your presence at the end of time, or will they truly endure into eternity?"

In such a quiet time as that, perhaps, Moses may have prayed, "Let the beauty and delightfulness and favor of the Lord our God be upon us; confirm and establish the work of our hands, yes, the work of our hands confirm and establish it" (Psalm 90:17, AMP).

I believe God gave the fourth commandment with this very sort of intimacy in mind. I've heard intimacy described as into-me-see. It is a point in my journey where I slow down enough so that the Lord can look into my life and see how I'm doing, and how I'm not doing…what needs to be touched…what needs to be done…where the spiritual shoes of my life are wearing thin. (See Psalm 139: 23–24.)

But this intimacy implies more than the Lord looking into my heart. Wonder of wonders, I get to look into *His* heart and life and see Him, too. He desires that I do so.

> Friendship with God is reserved for those who reverence
>   him.
> With them alone he shares the secrets of his promises.
> (Psalm 25:14, TLB)

I *need* to do this. I need to be reminded of what He wants me to do. I need to be reminded of His kindness and grace and goodness toward me.

Does God have a chance to look into your heart? *When?* Do you give Him time to do so? If not on a Sunday, then *when?* He knows we desperately need such times. It's as though our spirits were equipped with a rechargeable battery, and we simply run down after a while. The current becomes very weak, the light in our hearts becomes very dim, and it affects every other part of our lives. Every relationship. Every project. Everything we touch. God knows our need to be restored, and during that time of rest, that's what happens.

Do you have a particular place where you enjoy meeting the Lord—just the two of you? For me, there's no better place than on my knees beside the couch in my office. He has met me there so many times—He has comforted me and refreshed me and corrected me and spoken to me there so often that this particular corner of the world has become very dear to me.

One of my friends, however, isn't so wild about kneeling by a couch—he enjoys *walking* with the Lord. He feels closest to Jesus when he's out walking along a long stretch of country road. For him, that's where the real conversation begins. I've written before about the mother of a friend of mine, who slips down to a little creek on their property every day before breakfast. And with her back up against a California oak tree, she pours out her heart to God, and He pours out His heart to her.

Do you have a place where you love to meet Him? Any place will do, of course. History tells us that the eleventh-century monk Brother Lawrence felt closest to the Lord while he was in the kitchen, scrubbing pots and pans. He felt it was an interruption in his conversation with God when the bell rang for prayer time. God was so much a part of his kitchen duties that drying his hands and leaving for the chapel was just a bother. For you, that choice time with Him may be early in the morning, when the light of the new day sends little golden fingers into your room. Maybe it's during lunch hour, with half the day gone and half still to go. Maybe it's late at night after everyone has gone to bed. The Lord is ready when you are, where you are.

He just wants to be with you.

I don't think you and I could ever comprehend just how *much* He wants to be with us.

It may even be that you have to practice walking and talking with Him in the midst of other activities, as with Brother Lawrence. It might be a time when you get to work just a little bit harder to practice "praying without ceasing," and to relate everything you face that day to the love of God. For example, if you're in the boys' bedroom, then you pray for the boys, or remind the Lord that you're doing your best to raise them, but you need His wisdom, insight, and strength. If you're doing laundry, you pray for the person who owns the shirts or underwear you're folding. At the grocery store, you might thank the Lord for His constant provision, and perhaps remember those who don't have enough to eat, that God might somehow use you to minister to them.

Perhaps it's just making a conscious effort to be aware of the presence of God all day long. On this day—whatever day or portion of a day you designate as "Sabbath"—you make an honest attempt to keep God constantly in your thoughts.

I can remember the days of my courtship with Joyce, when we were both struggling to get through college. I'd be busy all the time, with studying, going to class, going to basketball practice, or getting my laundry done and my stuff organized in the dorm room. Yet all the time, Joyce would be on my mind. I would think of her a thousand times a day. Maybe they were just quick, fleeting thoughts, but they kept me going. And I could look forward to our dates on the weekends—no matter what we were doing—when we could just be together. I just wanted to be with her, going where she wanted to go, doing what she wanted to do, having an extended conversation with her about whatever she was thinking, feeling, planning, and dreaming. I wanted to listen to whatever she had to say. I wanted to concentrate on her.

That's a picture of our walk with the Lord. Through the week, though we are busy and pressed by responsibilities, we're thinking about Him whenever we can. We're shooting up little "arrow" prayers to Him and listening for His voice. But we always look forward to those longer, "Sabbath" times when we get to concentrate on Him, open our hearts to Him, and worship Him.

This, I believe, is the spirit of the fourth command. Yes, life can become incredibly hectic and complicated. We always have too much to do and not enough time to do it. But let's make sure that there is at least one day a week when we have extended time with Him. Because if we don't resolve it in our minds and write it on our calendars, the world will quickly swallow that time. Before we know it, the alarm clock will be ringing on Monday morning, and the opportunity will be lost.

It doesn't matter who you are, the work of life will never be "done." There will always be another letter to write, form to complete, errand to run, project to finish, or drawer to organize.

If you wait until you've "caught up" to have time with Him, it will never happen.

"Be still," He whispers, "and know that I am God" (Psalm 46:10).

But please remember this: *the path to Sabbath rest will always be a contested path.* Haven't you ever wondered why it seems so incredibly difficult to find these times with God in our life? Why it seems like such a chore to simply pick up your Bible or get down on your knees to pray? The enemy knows this path to the Sabbath will lead you to rest and righteousness and perspective and a reordering of your priorities. And Satan will try to thwart you. He doesn't want you to find that path. Never doubt it! He has a thousand ways to sidetrack and divert you.

Satan knows that if he keeps us striving in our own strength, the joy and sense of purpose in our lives will drain like oil out of a quarter-sized hole in your car's oil pan.

A Sabbath day is a life inventory day. It's like a shop owner inventorying his stock at the end of the week. God wants to do that inventory with us and show us what we have—and what we are lacking. Is there anything depleted? Have we given everything away? Are our shelves empty? That time with Him is the time to restore the inventory that's been expended through the week.

I have a mental image of the Lord with a pencil behind His ear and a clipboard in His hand, walking with me up and down the warehouse aisles of my soul. And He is saying, "Uh-huh, uh-huh. Oh, look at this, we're really down here, aren't we? The stocks are low."

Maybe we have a diminished supply of mercy or compassion. Maybe our endurance is down to almost bare shelving. Maybe our love has been given away until there is very little left, and our heart feels empty.

He is the One who can amply provide for whatever we need, whatever has been poured out in His service. As Paul wrote, "It is he who will supply all your needs from his riches in glory, because of what Christ Jesus has done for us" (Philippians 4:19, TLB).

He can help you inventory your relationships, too. He might say, "My daughter, your love relationship with your husband has been depleted. You need to take stock here. You need to let Me minister to you in this area." Or "My son, you've become cynical toward your boss. You're in danger of growing bitter! Let Me touch you and provide the love and the patience you will need for the coming week."

I guess it all comes down to this: Who's the manager of your life, anyway? Is He really Lord just because you call Him "Lord"? Do you give Him the opportunity as manager to evaluate where you're at and make changes and adjustments?

Because He loves us, He told us, "Remember the Sabbath day and keep it holy." When we do, we get to look back over our lives with no sense of regret or wasted time.

And you just may find yourself saying, "Lord, this is good. This is *really* good."

Lord, this kind of command ought to be one of the easiest to obey. Yet so often I find it the most difficult. You told us to

rest because we desperately need to. Lord, forgive me for my worrying, striving, manipulating, and scheming—as though everything somehow depended on me. Sin really is hard work, Lord. Taking things into my own hands has wearied me more than I can say. I look to You now as the One who restores my soul. I look to You as the One who said, "Come unto Me, all you that are weary and heavy-laden, and I will give you rest." That's what I want to do today, Lord. I want to be like Mary of Bethany, who sat quietly at Your feet...gazing into Your face, hanging on Your every word. The needs around her were pressing, too, but You told her she had made the best choice. I want to make the best choice, too.

And so today, Lord, I will listen for Your call and submit to Your tender command. In Jesus' name, amen.

"Honor your father and your mother,
that your days may be long upon the land
which the LORD your God is giving you."

EXODUS 20:12

CHAPTER 6

A COMMAND WITH A PROMISE

I stood nervously at the door and looked into the man's strained features. It was a face I had never seen before. Not even in a picture. Not even in my imagination. Yet it was like looking in a mirror.

Forty-something years of questions and apprehensions tumbled about in my mind. This was the first time I could ever remember seeing this man who called himself my father.

He invited Joyce and me into his tiny apartment. We hugged. He wept a little. We made an awkward attempt at small talk. As we began to speak of the past, he was very careful to take the blame for our family's breakup on himself. He'd gone away to the war, he told us in a quiet, hesitant voice. And when he came back to his wife and new baby, "things weren't the same." He didn't elaborate.

He looked into my eyes. "I know," he said slowly, "that you can never forgive me."

"Then I guess you really don't know me," I replied.

This encounter with my biological father took place some

years ago in Burnsville, Minnesota, after a nationwide search. It had been Joyce's idea. She had felt even more deeply than I had that there was something unfinished in my life. Joyce thought I should meet this man, look him in the eyes, and talk to him...if he was still alive.

I know that Joyce Mehl walks with the Lord, and when she urges me to consider something, I consider it. Truthfully, I hadn't felt any great need to see my father; I didn't feel that I was holding anything in my heart against him, or that I was troubled with bitterness or unforgiveness. But maybe she saw something I didn't see. Maybe she understood something, intuitively, that I hadn't understood.

So I agreed. And after much research, a thousand phone calls, and not a few miracles, she found him. We packed our bags for Minnesota. For me, it would be a living out of the fifth commandment in a way I had never expected or imagined.

If you had a list of the Ten Commandments evenly spaced on a sheet of binder paper and folded that sheet in half, top to bottom, the fifth commandment would be right at the fold.

This is a matter so important to the Lord that Scripture puts it squarely in the center of these commands. I don't think that was an accident. I believe these words are central to the Ten Commandments—and to life itself—because they affect *everything* about your life and mine. Just as the fifth commandment would appear at the fold of the piece of paper, so it also appears at the fold of our lives. In many ways, our destiny hinges on how we respond to this command. It affects our futures, it affects how we process the past, and it affects our right now—what God can and will do in our lives today.

Notice that this command is the only one of the Ten Commandments with a promise attached:

"Honor your father and your mother, *that your days may be long upon the land which the* LORD *your God is giving you.*" (Exodus 20:12)

Here again, so very clearly, we can see that the motive—the operative principle—behind the Ten Commandments is God's abiding love for us. They truly are the *tender* commandments.

Why should we honor father and mother? So that we might live. So that we might not be weighed down or taken captive by bitterness. So that we might not come to destruction. So that we might enjoy God's good gifts to us through the days of our lives. The Lord is saying, "Would you do this? Would you honor the father and mother that I gave you? And if you do, things will be well with you. If you are careful to do this, I will honor your life, I will bless your life, and I will extend your life. Because I love you, however, I must also warn you: if you violate this command, it will affect the whole fabric of your life."

Some of you might respond by saying, "How should I honor my parents?" Others of us have to get by the "why" before we can get to the "how." *Why* should I do this?

As I've mentioned, my father and mother went their separate ways when I was just a baby. Like so many others that I've counseled over the years, I too have had to face the pain and the emptiness of a dad who wasn't there for his little boy. He wasn't there to play catch with me. He wasn't there for my ball games or school activities. He wasn't there to encourage and comfort.

He had almost become "the man who never was"; my mother never mentioned his name to me once in her whole life.

Worst of all, I had to work through the feelings of rejection that began to surface in my adolescence. Maybe it was all because of me. Maybe I was the problem or reason for Mom and Dad's divorce. When you have time to wonder and no information to work with, you can begin to imagine all kinds of things.

Over the years, I've read Paul's words to the Thessalonians with an ache in my heart—an ache because of what I missed in my life. Paul wrote: "For you know that we dealt with each of you as a father deals with his own children, encouraging, comforting and urging you to live lives worthy of God, who calls you into his kingdom and glory" (1 Thessalonians 2:11–12, NIV).

We all long for a dad like that; a father who will encourage us and comfort us. A dad who will urge us to reach for the highest and best. When that's missing, it hurts. It aches. There's no denying it.

But I've learned something. I've learned that the one thing better than having such a father is *being* such a father. My dad wasn't there for me, but I can be there for my boys. My dad didn't encourage or comfort me, but by God's grace I can be a comforter and an encourager—not just to my own sons, but hopefully to many young men and women who feel lost and lonely as they grope their way along life's paths.

Even so, it's been an exercise of faith for me through the years to find ways to honor this man in my words and in my heart.

That's never been the case when I've thought about Mom. Preaching her funeral a few years ago was truly one of the highlights of my life. It was a joy to honor her memory before those who had gathered at the service. She modeled for me the value of pursuing "old paths," as the prophet spoke of in Jeremiah 6:16.

> Thus says the LORD:
> "Stand in the ways and see,
> and ask for the old paths, where the good way is,
> and walk in it;
> then you will find rest for your souls."

That was one of her favorite verses, and it became one of mine, too. I used it at her funeral and talked about her love of the "old paths" and old-fashioned things.

Not long after she died, I sat in her trailer house and looked up at her old roasting pan that she used when I was five or six years old. In her kitchen drawer was the same spatula that she used to serve cake and fudge. She still had the same old pots and pans and even the same jewelry—tiny brooches that had one or two red or green rhinestones missing. She had moved more than ten times since I was a little boy, but she always carried those things along.

I loved her old-fashioned gospel. I can still hear her testifying in church, "I thank God I'm saved, sanctified, and want to go all the way with Him." Mom was old-fashioned in that she thought salvation should make a difference in your life. If you still wanted what the world wanted, she would question your salvation. She loved the old-fashioned gospel because she knew it would change your heart.

She believed that to be saved and sanctified was to be "set

apart" for God's special use. Even her pots and pans were sanctified! One was set apart for roast, one was set apart for cake and fudge. And as far as she was concerned, a young man named Ron Mehl was set apart for God's glory. "Son," she'd tell me, "set your life apart for God's work and He'll bless you greatly."

My mom's Sunday roasts were better than any I've ever tasted when she cooked them in that old battered pot. What I've learned from Mom's old-fashioned ways is that if you'll put your life in God's hands, He'll cause you to turn out better than you ever thought you could.

I was very blessed to have a mom who loved the Lord and loved me very much. Yet you may be reading this chapter and thinking, *This command obviously isn't something that's going to apply to me, because I don't have the kind of parents who should be honored. I certainly don't want to honor them and don't intend to. If this author knew what I've been through in my life—if he knew the scars and the grief and the abuse—there's no way in the world he would expect this commandment to apply to me.*

Maybe I do know about a few of those things. Yet the fact is, the commandment applies to all of us. It applies to those who have good, godly, loving parents, and to those who don't. The Lord didn't list any exceptions, exemptions, or special considerations. And just to make sure we understand how profoundly this command applies to us, He made sure it was repeated in the New Testament:

> "Honor your father and mother," which is the first commandment with promise: "that it may be well with you and that you may live long on the earth." (Ephesians 6:2–3)

It applies to all of us. And please hear this: No matter what has happened to us in the past, God is interested in our *right now.*

He wants to change your heart and mine right now. Not tomorrow.

He wants to walk with us and fellowship with us right now. Not later on, after we "get things straightened out."

He wants to teach us and bless us right now. Not on some mythical future day when we're "more prepared" or "have our act together."

He wants to protect us from destructive thoughts and attitudes right now. And right now, if I settle this matter of honoring my parents, I can be a different person. A son or daughter who forgives from the heart can be a different kind of parent to his or her own children. An honorable parent. A parent free from bitterness. A parent—and a child—that the heavenly Father can bless and use in unimaginable ways.

No, God doesn't close His eyes or ignore the pain parents sometimes inflict on their own children. He places great value on the home and holds mothers and fathers accountable for their parenting. In Matthew 18:6 (NASB), the Lord Jesus said very sternly, "But whoever causes one of these little ones who believe in Me to stumble, it is better for him that a heavy millstone be hung around his neck, and that he be drowned in the depth of the sea."

The Lord understands the hurt and the pain many children endure, and it does not escape His notice. He takes it very, very seriously. He knows that when a person is abused or neglected at home, it affects him or her greatly, down to the very core. Yet even knowing and understanding these things more deeply and intimately than you and I ever could in a lifetime, His Word still teaches us: "Honor your father and mother…that it may go well with you."

So how, then, do I do that? How do I honor my mother and father?

By Loving Them

Love, someone said, is best spelled T-I-M-E. You love someone when you spend time with that person. "Well," you say, "I don't really care to spend time with my parents. I think they love making me feel miserable."

That may be. Honoring them by your presence may be a difficult thing to do. Tracking down my father and flying across the country to meet him and be with him wasn't an easy thing for me to do. There were times when my flesh rebelled at the thought. There were times when I felt I'd rather face another chemotherapy treatment than face that. But more than needing to do what I wanted to do, I needed to obey the Lord. Why? Because the Lord has said to me, "If you love Me, keep My commandments. If you keep My commandments, you will abide in My love, just as I have kept My Father's commandments and abide in His love" (John 14:15; 15:10).

That's the best reason I can think of for obeying the Ten Commandments. I want to abide in His love. I don't want to live or abide in any other place for any other reason. For me, life means walking and talking and ministering while I'm being swept along in the main current of His love. And that means I need to obey, even when the obeying is difficult.

Maybe you'd love to spend more time with your older parents, but they live far away. It's not always easy to break away from work or responsibilities to spend a whole day—or three or four days—with them. Yet it's been said that you only really love someone when you sacrifice for them. The Lord proved His love by laying down His life. One of the best ways to show our love for our parents is to endure some of that inconvenience and sacrifice for their sakes. If you have taken the time and trouble to set aside other obligations and commitments to be in their presence, that is certainly showing honor toward them. And God is well pleased.

But there are certainly other ways to show love and affection when travel is impossible. It may be as simple as a handwritten note or card, even when it's not a birthday or a holiday. It may be just picking up the phone in the middle of the day and saying, "How's it going? I was thinking about you, and I want you to know that I love you."

The truth is, you really can't say you love someone without being willing to give up something for them. Time and energy are two of our most precious commodities...but then, sometimes we're rewarded for that sacrifice in ways we never expected.

I remember when I was a kid, my mom would always make me eat peas and spinach. Especially spinach. I'd even pretend to throw up so I didn't have to eat it. It still isn't my favorite food by a long stretch. It seemed like Mom was feeding me that stuff at every opportunity. At the time, I was sure she was doing it out of spite.

A couple of years before she died, I visited Mom in the convalescent home. Since it was lunchtime, I took the opportunity to be with her and feed her. You'll never guess what was on her plate. Spinach!

Ah, sweet revenge!

Toward the end of her life, Mom had diabetes and all she wanted to eat were sweet things—ice cream and cake and pudding. The good stuff. Spinach—especially canned, institutional spinach—was the last thing she wanted to see. I thought, *All right, I'll teach you for persecuting me!* So I held up a spoonful of spinach, and she turned up her little nose at it, as if to say, "No thanks!" I wish you could have seen how cute she looked. We both broke out laughing.

As she began to cast longing eyes over at the dessert on her tray, I said, "Oh no, you don't! I can't believe this is happening! I had this 'clean your plate' deal drummed into my head for years, so what goes around comes around. You're eating this! Watch, Mom, here comes the airplane."

When I was very small, I remembered her doing that airplane deal with the spoon to coax my mouth open. She'd say, "Look at this little airplane, honey. It's coming in for a landing." And boom, she'd shove it into my mouth. I can't imagine why I fell for that and gave landing rights for an airborne load of that green stuff, but I did. (Even now, every time I hear a plane fly by overhead I want to cover my mouth with my hand for protection!)

You learn amazing things at home. But of course, all of us know that when it comes to really loving someone, it isn't because everything they've ever done is "worthy" of love and affection. They're not perfect. My mom wasn't perfect, either. Before she became a Christian I'm sure there were things in her life that must have hurt my father deeply and contributed to his leaving. No, she wasn't perfect. But the last time I checked, *none* of us are.

But I can tell you this: there are no more potent words in the world to a parent's ears than the three little words "I love you." Nothing else even comes close.

These may be words we said a lot as kids. "I love you, Mom. I love you, Dad." Then what happens? Kids get older and more "sophisticated." They don't do that mushy stuff anymore. Because, of course, it isn't cool to have your dad hug you—especially in public. It isn't really the classy thing to do. So you kind of stiffen up. You communicate with your body language, "This is baby stuff. I don't want to be touched anymore."

When those words "I love you" and the accompanying physical affection are denied to a parent, it creates a desolation within the soul that sometimes can't be described.

Most dads that I know long to be loved and admired by their kids. There's something in our masculine soul that wants to be a hero to our sons and daughters—even if we're not a hero to anyone else. When the kids are little, it's easy to step into that role. Sometimes, just walking through the front door in the evening makes you a hero!

"It's DAD! Daddy's home! Daddy's home!"

A friend of mine told me how he would ride the city bus home at night and walk the last half mile home down a winding road. Sometimes his little son and daughter would run to the halfway point and wait for him to come around the corner so they could hold his hands and escort him the rest of the way home. He told me that no conquering Roman general ever felt more honored and esteemed than he did.

I remember a particular conversation with my son Ron Jr. when he was in junior high. We had been sitting together, gabbing about a myriad of things. We talked about school, about the youth group at church, and about how he felt he was coming along in hockey. Girls were still a taboo subject at that time, but he was open to talking about what he might do and be in the future.

Suddenly I tossed a question at him from out of the blue.

"Are you proud to be a Mehl, son?"

I don't know what made me ask such a thing in that moment. To be honest, I had probably been feeling a little insecure at that time of my life. I'd probably reasoned that if there was one person in the world who would value me and give me a little affirmation, it was my son.

But Ron didn't say a word.

He couldn't give me an answer—which really was an answer in itself. His silence shook me a little. It was a revelation to me. He couldn't look me in the eyes and say, "I'm proud to be your son, Dad." Could he have misunderstood me? I asked the question a different way. "Is it difficult being a pastor's kid, Ron? Are you embarrassed about what I do?"

Suddenly, the silence seemed very, very heavy.

My son looked away from me and couldn't find anything to say. I quickly let him off the hook and changed the subject. We went on talking about this and that. But in my heart, I was wounded; those were difficult moments for me. I wanted my son to be proud of me. I wanted him to say, "There's no dad in the world like you."

Neither of us ever forgot that moment…as I would learn later.

I never asked either of my boys that question again. But in the back of my mind, I always wondered. I began to realize that it wasn't the most wonderful thing in the world to say to kids at school, "Oh yeah, my dad's the pastor of a church." From that time on, through all the following years, I wondered if my boys were just a little embarrassed that I was their father. They never said anything about it, but it pained me to wonder what kind of ridicule they were having to deal with. Would they ever come to the place where they were proud of who I was and what I did?

A number of years later, when I least expected it, the answer came. It was during the celebration of the twentieth anniversary of our pastorate at the church. A "special guest speaker," unnamed, had been announced for the Sunday evening service. For weeks I tried to pry that information out of Chuck Updike, our associate pastor and my dear friend. Chuck was overseeing the anniversary plans, but he stonewalled me. I couldn't get so much as a hint out of him about our special speaker.

Who would they bring? One of our old professors? Another pastor? I couldn't imagine.

On the night of the celebration, Joyce and I were escorted to our front-row seats in the sanctuary, which was filled to capacity with those we had loved and served for the past twenty years. To say it was an emotional time for us would be a serious understatement. But we were completely unprepared for what happened next. When the time came, Chuck stepped to the microphone and said, "I'd like to introduce to you our speaker for the evening…*Ron Mehl*."

Suddenly every eye in the sanctuary seemed to turn toward us. I felt the blood drain right out of my face, and my hands began to sweat. My first thought was, *Why in the world would Chuck do something like this to me?* My next thought was, *I don't have anything prepared! What am I going to say?*

The mystery speaker, Ron Mehl *Junior*, hesitated just long enough to make Ron Mehl Senior, squirm; then he walked to the platform with a big grin on his face. When I saw who was going to speak, I put my face into my hands and began to weep. Ron, now a college graduate, had never been in front of the church or spoken publicly in his life.

And to think he would step up in front of 2,500 people at our anniversary service overwhelmed me.

"A long time ago," Ron began, "Dad asked me a question. He asked me, 'Are you proud to be a Mehl? Are you embarrassed about what I do?' Well, you know how kids are…they want their dad to be a pro basketball player or a rocket scientist. But at that time I really didn't know what being a pastor was or what a pastor did. I didn't tell him I was embarrassed, but…I couldn't look at him and tell him I wasn't."

Ron went on to describe what it was like to be used in so many illustrations from the pulpit. He would get out of Sunday school, and someone from the first service would say, "Boy, your dad's been talking about you again. Wait'll you hear what he said this time!"

At that point Ron smiled and said, "I think turnabout is fair play, don't you? I've got a few stories of my own to tell." With that, he hauled out a massive three-ring binder. (Thank goodness he was kidding!)

As he wrapped up his twenty-five-minute talk, Ron said, "I want to say that I couldn't be any more proud of my parents than I am, and I know that goes for my brother as well. I wouldn't want them to do anything else than to pastor this church." And then he looked at Joyce and me and said, "Thanks for loving us and making us proud to be your sons. We love you, Mom and Dad."

What did that mean to me? It was a highlight of my life. And I can tell you this: when Ron Mehl is an old man and my teeth are falling out and I can't see anymore, I will still love to hear those big sons of ours say, "I love you, Dad." There is no better way to honor your father or mother. These are words that have the power to sustain a parent to his or her dying day.

I remember some years ago walking into St. Vincent's Hospital to visit a pastor friend, recovering from very serious surgery. When I walked into his room, I saw his huge seventeen-year-old son actually lying in the bed alongside his dad, with the mom sitting in a chair next to the bed. All of them were there together, laughing and joking. I stood in the doorway for a moment and thought, *Wow*. I was moved.

This big kid was not too "sophisticated" or cool to say, "This is my dad, I love him, and I don't care who knows it." He wanted to be close to him and identify with him, and that closeness meant more to that young man than what anybody else in the world might have thought about it.

When his son left the room, I said, "You must really love that big guy a lot." He said, "Ron, every day of my boy's life I've told him I love him. And you know something? Every day of his life he tells me how much he loves me. *Nothing* means more to me."

I remember the last few days before my friend Bill Estep's death. Bill was hospitalized with an inoperable brain tumor, and in those last few days before his passing he was always surrounded by his six kids. What an impressive family. Incredibly attractive daughters and big, strong sons. This is one of those families that, whenever you're around them, you think "This is the way it ought to be." They were always loving one another, hugging one another.

I still remember walking into his room on one of his last mornings. The night before, *all six kids* had slept in his bedroom with him. Don't ask me how! There were bodies everywhere… sleeping on the floor, on pillows, hanging over the side of the bed, just to be close to Dad.

On another occasion, I'd gone to the Estep home to pray with Bill. While we were in the family room talking, one of his girls came through the front door. And the moment she stepped across the threshold, she began to run. She ran all the way through the house, jumped up on the couch, hugged her dad's neck, and kissed and kissed him. When it dawned on her that I was there, she looked up for a moment and said, "Oh, Pastor, excuse me." But she just went on hugging her dad and cuddling with him. She wasn't a bit embarrassed or ashamed by what anybody else thought. Obviously it meant the world to her. It certainly meant the world to him.

As I reflect on that scene, and a hundred others like it, I'm convinced of one thing. Life is like a vapor, so you'd better be loving now. While you can.

All of us know there's nothing quite like hearing your son or your daughter say "I love you." Have you ever been attacked by a little one in the hallway, with those little arms and legs wrapping tightly around your leg and clinging to you like a barnacle on a rock? Have you ever heard the words, "I'm not going to let you go, Daddy." "I'm not going to let you loose, Mommy."

Nothing in the world compares to that. You can heap up all the honors and acclaim and awards you want. You can talk about Olympic gold medals, or promotions at work, or writing bestsellers, or winning the Publisher's Clearinghouse grand prize. Nothing compares to the fierce love of your own child.

If you as a parent are the recipient of such love, value it, cultivate it, guard it, and return it with all your heart and soul and might.

If you are the child—whether you're fourteen or forty—remember: There is no better way to honor your father and mother.

But there is one additional way to keep the fifth commandment in relationship with your parents.

By Forgiving Them

Now that I'm over half a century old, I've finally discovered something. I've discovered that in most cases, my mom did what she thought was right when she was raising me. At the time, I thought, "This can't be right. You don't like me. You hate me. You're being too hard on me. You're trying to make my life miserable." Now I realize she usually knew something I didn't: that this really was the best thing for me.

When we told our boys no, we did it because we loved them. There wasn't any question about that. Yes, we all make mistakes. Don't be afraid to admit it. Yes, we have to make tough decisions. And here's what to say when you're facing one of those decisions. Let's say you are talking to your young son. You say, "Son, this is a decision I have to make. God holds me responsible to make it. You may disagree with me, and—five or ten years from now—I may have to apologize and say, 'You were right and I was wrong.' But right now, son, I'm doing what I think is right and best for you."

But there may have been instances in your life when your parents certainly did not have your best interest in mind. You may have been hurt or abused or neglected because of their self-ishness. How do you honor such a parent? How do you walk in obedience to the fifth command? By forgiving him. By forgiving her. Forgiving means "to let go," or "to send away."

But you say, "Ron, you have no idea what I've been through. How can I just let that go? You don't know what you're talking about."

No, I really don't know what you've been through. But I do know something of what Jesus went through. In the book of Isaiah, some two thousand years before Christ was born in Bethlehem, the prophet was given a glimpse into what this Servant of the Lord would endure:

We despised him and rejected him—a man of sorrows, acquainted with bitterest grief. We turned our backs on him and looked the other way when he went by. He was despised and we didn't care.... He was wounded and bruised for our sins. He was beaten that we might have peace; he was lashed—and we were healed.... God laid on him the guilt and sins of every one of us.

He was oppressed and he was afflicted, yet he never said a word. He was brought as a lamb to the slaughter; and as a sheep before her shearers is dumb, so he stood silent before the ones condemning him. From prison and trial they led him away to his death.... He was buried like a criminal in a rich man's grave; but he had done no wrong, and had never spoken an evil word. (Isaiah 53:3, 5–9, TLB)

Jesus knew what it meant to be ill-treated, abused, and falsely accused. He knew what it meant to have loving words thrown right back in His face. He knew how it felt to be betrayed and abandoned by someone close to Him. He knew what it was to be so misunderstood by His own family that at one point they tried to have Him committed. Yet He forgave. He loved. He laid down His life.

When it comes to true forgiveness, never forget this: *The innocent party almost always pays.* The one who forgives, the one who has been offended, is usually the one who must pay the price. But it is a price worth paying. You can't believe how much it pays to forgive. It is light out of darkness. It is life out of death.

I have always believed that the vast majority of ground Satan holds in any believer's life is a simple unwillingness to forgive. And remember, Ephesians 4:26–27 tells us that the enemy's very first foothold in our soul begins with harboring one single night of unresolved anger. With that beachhead in a Christian's life, Satan brings in the troops, the helicopters, and the heavy artillery. He digs in, fortifies his position, and becomes very, very difficult to dislodge. Why does he do this? Because he knows very well that bitterness and unforgiveness have the power to lock up your life in the past. As far as the kingdom of heaven is concerned you might as well be off the planet, because God can neither use you nor bless you.

In the end, even though the price may be steep, the one who forgives will know and experience the mighty blessings of God Almighty on his or her life. And how much is that worth? How do you calculate the value of that?

While Jesus taught us that forgiveness should be a daily way of life for all of us, the fact is, you couldn't honor your parents more than to forgive them. They may be guilt-ridden and full of remorse and regret, or they may be oblivious to your pain and hard as nails. They may recognize that they have miserably failed, or they may shrug it off. Nevertheless, *forgiveness is powerful.* It will change their lives…and it will change yours.

That day in the little apartment in Burnsville, Minnesota, I remember looking at my dad and saying, "How could I not forgive you? If the Lord has forgiven me and doesn't hold anything against me after all I've done, how could I ever hold anything against you?

"Dad, listen to me. I don't know everything about the past and I don't want to. But I forgive you."

When I said those words, tears sprang into his eyes. I could almost hear the sounds of a key being turned in a lock and a jail door swinging open. I remembered the Lord's words, "The Spirit of the LORD is upon Me, because He has anointed Me to preach the gospel to the poor; He has sent Me to heal the brokenhearted" and "to proclaim liberty to the captives." (Luke 4:18)

I could see in his eyes that he experienced *release* in that moment. And in a strange way, I guess I did, too. Joyce had been right (as she usually is). I sensed a completion in my own heart in an area that had long been under lock and key. To my knowledge, I hadn't held any bitterness—but that whole area of my heart had been tucked down in the bottom of a deep freeze. After that moment, the frost melted.

Just six months later, he passed away.

Maybe it all comes down to this: How much do you want the Lord to use your life? How available do you really want to be when the Holy Spirit looks for someone to pick up and use for His purposes in this generation?

I'll tell you this: I want to be used. As long as I have breath in my body, I want the Lord to use me for the glory of His name. Years and years ago, I remember saying to my mother, "Mom, I want to be a blessing." And my mom said, "Then son, be *bless-able*." And I know what she meant. What she meant was, "Son, if you want to be a blessing, then give God a reason to bless you."

She might have also said, "Son, don't ever give God a reason to *remove* His hand of blessing from you and move it somewhere else."

Because I want His blessing and I want to be a blessing, I am willing to obey…even when it hurts. The hurt, after all, will quickly pass away. The smile of God is forever.

Lord Jesus, it moves me to consider Your respect and love for Your earthly parents. During the most difficult, painful,

stressful hour of Your life, Your deep concern was for the welfare of Your mother, who stood at the foot of Your cross. Help me to live and walk in your tender compassion. Help me to remember that as I seek my mother and father's earthly and eternal welfare, Your promised blessings will come my way.

And so today, Lord, I humbly receive the guidance You have offered from the parents You've given me. In Jesus' name, amen.

"You shall not murder."

Exodus 20:13

REMOVING THE SEEDS OF MURDER

SATAN SEEKS A FOOTHOLD

God knows very well how far humanity has fallen.

He knows (who better?) what kind of world this has become because of man's rebellion. You and I react with shock to the stories of murder and mayhem on the morning news. But none of it is "news" to Him. He knew the morning news last night. He knew it ten thousand years ago. He knows what the headlines will be tomorrow. He has always known.

He knew every act of violence that would be perpetuated on this old earth in the moment when He looked at Adam in the garden and said, "What have you done?" And He knew even then what the only possible remedy would be…and what that remedy would cost Him.

He has seen it all before. There was a time when the earth became so filled with violence and bloodshed that he plucked one godly family out of the mess and sent a worldwide flood to wipe the planet clean and begin again.

The sad fact is, when the evil in man's heart is unchecked,

God knows that men and women will simply destroy themselves. He understands all too clearly the roots of murder that grow in the human heart. And were it not for His intervening grace and restraining hand, man could very well have eliminated himself from the world and ended his own history—probably a long time ago.

Yet God, in His love, has not allowed that to happen. And that is why, when He met with Moses on the mountain before the eyes of the watching nation, He included these four weighty words among His ten commands: *"You shall not murder."*

Are we approaching, once again, the way it was in the times of Noah?

By the time a child grows up in America, he or she will have viewed tens of thousands of murders and acts of violence on television and in the movies. If that wasn't enough, we can now "act out" violent inclinations with a video game or on a computer screen. In the new game Carmageddon, for instance, drivers get points for running over pedestrians—including little old ladies with walkers. Good fun, huh? In Postal, players pretend to be berserk postal employees who get points for killing innocent bystanders, including women and children. "Listen to victims moan and beg for mercy," reads the promotion on the Postal Web site. "Execute them if they get on your nerves."[1]

When it comes to violence and killing, our culture seems to shrug and say, "That's just the way it is." And there is reason to believe so. You can't watch the news and not hear about some parent killing or wounding his or her own child…or vice versa.

What makes a fourteen-year-old boy in a small Kentucky town walk up to a high school prayer meeting and calmly gun down his fellow students, killing three and wounding five?

What makes a man walk into a post office and shoot five of his fellow workers at close range—colleagues with whom he had worked for years?

What makes a mom in Florida push her own eighteen-month-old son out of the window of a speeding car onto the median strip?

We live in an angry world. Drive-by shootings are the order of the day. Killing has become something passionless and cool, with no accompanying sense of remorse. There are wars on innocent civilians, so-called mercy killings, and countless abortions, yet many take no offense. Civil liberties groups rouse themselves to heights of passion to preserve our "rights" to kill…whether taking our own lives with a pharmacist's lethal prescription or killing little babies just as they emerge from the womb. (Isn't it ironic that the pressing "civil liberties" issues of the day should revolve around the question *How can we kill more people?*)

Now, you might be saying, "I've never murdered anyone. And for that matter, I've never committed adultery, so why am I wasting my time with this stuff?" But before you check out on me, look at the Lord's words in Matthew 5 for a moment. It seems that many in His day had read these commandments and were inclined to check out, too. But Jesus caught them (and us) up short when He said these words:

> "You have heard that it was said to those of old, 'You shall
> not murder,' and whoever murders will be in danger of
> the judgment. But I say to you that whoever is angry with

his brother without a cause shall be in danger of the judgment. And whoever says to his brother, 'Raca!' shall be in danger of the council. But whoever says, 'You fool!' shall be in danger of hell fire." (Matthew 5:21–22)

It strikes me that saying "Raca!" (Empty-Head) and "Fool!" to someone comes close to writing off that person altogether. What we're really saying is, "This person doesn't even deserve to be alive. I don't want anything to do with this person. As far as I'm concerned, he's dead…and I really wouldn't mind pushing him over the edge."

That is murder in the heart. And that is where it all starts.

So how does this sixth commandment reflect the love of God? In what way is "You shall not murder" one of His *tender* commandments? Why would God give us this warning? Because He knows that when I love Him above all else and put Him first in my life, I will not injure anyone. It will not be in my heart to offend, slander, hurt, humiliate, destroy, or write anyone off. Instead, I will have His heart toward men, women, and children.

But what about the blind, empty-headed fools of the world? What about those who have made themselves my enemies?

I will love them. Just as He loved me and went to the cross for me when I was a fool and blind and an enemy of God.

The Lord tells us, "I know something about you. I know how you tick. And I know that when you love me with all your heart, when My life is alive in you through My Holy Spirit, that love of Mine is going to gush through the pipes of your heart and you're going to be a loving person. And in that loving nature, you're going to experience life, joy, and peace." That's not *exactly* what Paul said in Romans, but it's close!

> Now hope does not disappoint, because the love of God has been poured out in our hearts by the Holy Spirit who was given to us.… May the God of hope fill you with all joy and peace as you trust in him, so that you may overflow with hope by the power of the Holy Spirit. (Romans 5:5; 15:13, NIV)

What, then, is the real source of this commandment? What causes people to murder?" Matthew 5:21–22 tells us the source very plainly.

According to Jesus, murder begins with *anger*.

People become very angry, so angry that they kill. Yes, to our sorrow, some literally do kill people. But in the Sermon on the Mount, we learn that killing really begins with what we say. ("Fool!" "Empty-head!") Murder begins with seeds of hatred and anger that we allow to take root in our hearts. We say, "If looks could kill…" But in a sense, they can. Anger and hatred are murderous things; they distort our eyes and our countenances, so that our very faces reflect death.

Married couples will get in a fight and say, "I don't like you. I never have liked you. Frankly, I don't even know why I married you." When couples get into terrible fights like these, Scripture has this counsel: Ephesians 4:26–27 (NIV) says, "'In your anger do not sin': Do not let the sun go down while you are still angry, and do not give the devil a foothold."

Don't go to bed angry! Don't go to bed without dealing with

the issues. Don't close your eyes in sleep without working through these things. Why? Because verse 27 says that if you let the anger simmer overnight, you're going to give the enemy of your soul a toehold, or beachhead, in your life. You're going to give him a "place" in your soul, and from that place he will be able to direct his destructive activities in order to bring you and your family to disaster. Overnight, he has the opportunity to plant the terrible seeds of murder in your unguarded heart.

Never forget: Your soul has a bitter adversary who *wants* to see such disaster in your life. Scripture warns us to "be self-controlled and alert. Your enemy the devil prowls around like a roaring lion looking for someone to devour" (1 Peter 5:8, NIV). Unresolved anger draws Satan to your life and to your home like raw meat draws a shark. And he will devour you, your marriage, and your family if you let those seeds of murderous anger take root in your life.

Verses 26 and 27 speak of giving Satan a "foothold." Have you ever seen rock climbers or mountain climbers scale an almost vertical surface just by finding a place to set one toe or grab hold with two fingers? Giving Satan, "the father of lies," a toehold in your life and in your home will bring death to everything that is precious to you.

God knows what a toehold of anger can do—especially within a family. If we have any doubts, we have only to go back in time and see what transpired in the very first family.

In the course of time Cain brought some of the fruits of the soil as an offering to the LORD. But Abel brought fat portions from some of the firstborn of his flock. The

LORD looked with favor on Abel and his offering, but on Cain and his offering he did not look with favor. So Cain was very angry, and his face was downcast.

Then the LORD said to Cain, "Why are you angry? Why is your face downcast? If you do what is right, will you not be accepted? But if you do not do what is right, sin is crouching at your door; it desires to have you, but you must master it."

Now Cain said to his brother Abel, "Let's go out to the field." And while they were in the field, Cain attacked his brother Abel and killed him. (Genesis 4:3–8, NIV)

How much God loves us! He tried to reason with Cain. He tried to reassure and comfort this disappointed, angry man. And finally, He gave him a serious warning. But Cain had nurtured the anger and bitterness in his heart for so long that even *God* standing in the pathway before him wasn't going to stop him. He walked right around God to kill his only brother.

As in all the issues of our lives, Jesus deals with the *root* of this commandment, not just the fruit. He is not content to trim off the nettles and poison oak in our lives close to the ground. He wants to uproot the whole poisonous weed. And He tells us that the root of murder is anger…hateful, people-dishonoring anger.

We, like the Pharisees, would rather deal with externals. "Well, I've never shot or stabbed anyone. I've never put cyanide in anyone's Tylenol or clubbed anyone from behind with a brass candlestick like they do in the old movies." But the Lord wants to talk about *internal things*. He wants to talk about what's really happening in my heart. And He knows that long before I would club anyone over the head in an effort to end his life, I may begin the process with my thoughts and then take it even further with my words. Don't entertain any false notions here. Words *do* hurt. Words *can* kill.

Back when I was in grade school, there was a boy named Dennis who would never leave me alone. Whenever he saw me, he would laugh and say, "Look! Here comes Big Ears Mehl." I can't tell you how much that bothered me. I was shy and insecure anyway, and was probably doing my best to find some reason why I might be a worthwhile person. And then Dennis started tossing that stuff at me every day. Suddenly my ears felt as big as Dumbo's. I wanted to hide. I wanted to die.

You might say that part of me did die. The light went out in my eyes. My spirit was quenched. This was a killing thing. My mother could tell something was happening just by looking at me. One afternoon when I came dragging into the house, Mom said, "What's wrong, son? What's going on? Why are you so unhappy?" So I told her about the boy at school who kept calling me names like Big Ears Mehl.

To this day, I remember my mom saying, "Son, you just remember this: 'Sticks and stones may break my bones, but words will never hurt me.'"

I know Mom wanted to help. And I really did want to believe what she told me. So when Dennis saw me the next day and yelled, "Big Ears! Big Ears! Here's Big Ears Mehl," I took my mom's advice and told him, "Sticks and stones may break my bones, but words will never hurt me."

But do you know what I discovered that day? You've probably discovered it, too. Mom was wrong. Words *do* hurt. Words *do* cause deep pain and discouragement. Words not only break my bones, they *crush* my bones. Solomon wrote: "A cheerful heart is good medicine, but a crushed spirit dries up the bones" (Proverbs 17:22, NIV).

Words can devastate a person's life. They can wipe a smile off a face. They can take the sparkle out of an eye. They can steal hope out of a heart. They can sour a friendship of many years. They can cast a shadow over a beautiful day. They can quench those little sparks of fun and joy and laughter and tenderness that make life worth living. James wrote, "But no man can tame the tongue. It is an unruly evil, full of deadly poison" (James 3:8).

God knows that without Him, we will wound people. We will make our lives and the lives of those around us miserable. Without Him, we're going to hurt people. Without Him, we're going to be an angry, impatient, self-centered people. Unless He heals me and touches me, there's no way I could do anything but be offensive and ultimately hurt the people I love most.

Let me tell you about a lady—a strikingly beautiful woman—who went to her pastor for counseling. During the course of the appointment, she told him that she was having difficulty responding romantically to her husband because, she said, "I'm so unattractive."

The pastor was thinking to himself, *You've got to be kidding!*

So then she told this story. As a teenager, acne covered her face. She had crooked teeth and wore Coke-bottle glasses. But an amazing thing happened. She turned fourteen and began to develop faster than other girls her age. One day she was on her way to school and the big man on campus saw her walking to class. She felt his eyes on her as she walked, and he spoke to one of his friends so that she could overhear him.

"Woo-eee. Wouldja look at her!" he said. "Put a bag over her head and she'd be terrific."

In time, she outgrew the bad complexion. Braces straightened her teeth, and contact lenses replaced the thick glasses. She became a beautiful young woman, and everyone knew it.

Everyone but her.

The words that young man had so carelessly, hatefully spoken had crushed her spirit and strangled any confidence or feelings of self-worth she might have begun to develop. So much so that *twenty-five years later* she couldn't respond to the admiration of her husband and kept thinking, "All I really need to do to be attractive is wear a big bag over my head."

Hateful words and unresolved anger in the heart can not only destroy others, it can destroy the one who harbors it. It is murderous whether directed at someone else or directed at yourself. Ten or eleven years ago, I remember leaning over the bed of a person in the hospital who had tried to commit suicide. He had slashed his wrists three or four times on both arms, and yet had survived. This young man looked up at me from his bed and said, "You know something? I've heard about other people committing suicide, but I said I could never, ever do that. But…here I am."

Have you ever said something like that? I can remember saying it. I can remember saying to myself, *I could never bring myself to put a gun to my head and pull the trigger or slash my wrists. I could never do that.* But I don't say that anymore. The reason I don't say that anymore is because I've observed again and again the terrible, tragic power that results from long-held anger and frustration. If that deadly anger in my life or yours is not dealt with, it will continue to grow and grow and, at some point, it will manifest itself. It will bear fruit in a way that, frankly, will be shocking. We will find ourselves saying or doing something we never dreamed we would ever say or do.

And I know that if Ron Mehl gave the Destroyer a foothold in his life, and that if he carried toxic anger in his heart long enough, he would be capable of doing *anything*…and the Lord knows that, too.

That's why the Lord says, "Put Me first, because if you don't, you'll hurt yourself and others. Instead of being a bearer of life, you will be a bearer of death and destruction."

In the place of these damaging tendencies of our flesh, God wants to cultivate a much different garden in our hearts and lives. That's why, from my perspective, Galatians 5:22 answers so much of this. God wants us to develop within us—by His Spirit—those healing qualities of love, joy, peace, patience, kindness, goodness, faithfulness, gentleness, and self control. Because when you are filled with the love of God, God's love is the very thing that comes forth from your life.

This morning I woke up at about 3:00 A.M. and couldn't go back to sleep. I went into the bathroom to brush my teeth and an amazing thing happened. I took the tube of toothpaste, squeezed it, and do you know what came out? *Toothpaste*. I kid you not. It wasn't mashed potatoes. It wasn't Jello. It wasn't scented topical muscle rub. Just white, minty toothpaste.

And God knows that when I put Him first in my life, the first thing that will come out of my life when I am put under pressure will be His love. When my life has been filled with the love, peace, long-suffering, patience, and kindness of God, then when I am squeezed by people, circumstances, challenges, troubles, and problems, the Lord knows that out of my life and out of your life will come expressions of His love and His grace.

WHY WE BECOME ANGRY

The Lord said that if I am angry and hateful to someone, I am a murderer in my heart. So how do I deal with that? What are the causes of anger and what do I do with them? Why do we become angry?

Because We Get Hurt

If you get your finger slammed in a door, let me tell you, it hurts—and someone is going to hear about it. When we get hurt or offended, we can become very frustrated and angry. It begins to simmer deep within (just as it did with Cain), but in time it explodes.

What in the world would make a guy walk into a McDonald's in San Diego and begin to shoot everyone in sight? What would make someone do that? You're talking about a person who allowed anger and hurt to seep into the deep cavities of his soul. And because it was never dealt with, it began to grow and seethe. Over time, those toxins became explosive. Unstable. All it took was a little spark to touch off a major, life-destroying explosion.

God knows that anger—unchecked and unrestrained—will

eventually manifest itself. And unless I deal with that, and God does something to touch me, heal me, and deliver me, I'll hurt someone else because I am hurt.

Because We Get in a Hurry and Become Impatient

It doesn't take very much to get us angry on certain days, does it? All of us know that if you wait on a freeway long enough, you can become pretty hot. If you are forced to wait in a line (when you weren't expecting to), you can grow fangs just standing there. *What is this? What's with this store? What's with these people? Why can't they get out their checkbooks BEFORE the total is rung up? Why are they moving so cotton-picking slow?*

We become angry because we want our "rights." We want what we want when we want it. We tell ourselves that we "deserve" this or that, and we ought to have it right now!

How do I deal with this kind of restless, impatient anger?

First, I need to think before I act. You can't believe how important this is. If Cain had taken a long walk in the orchard or sat by a stream for half an hour or so instead of calling his brother out into the field, how different his life would have been. Instead of being a marked man and an outcast for the rest of his life, he would have had a family to come home to that night. He would have had company around the evening fire. He would have had a brother at his side as they built a new world together.

But it was all lost in a moment.

James said it very simply: "Let every man be swift to hear, slow to speak, slow to wrath" (James 1:19). You can pay a counselor any amount of money, but you'll never find any advice better than that. Thomas Jefferson affirmed that when he was angry, he would force himself to count to ten. And when he was *really* angry, he'd count to a hundred. There are times when I just count and count until I run out of numbers, because I know that if I stopped counting, I would end up being very sorry.

Proverbs 13:16 (TLB) says, "A wise man thinks ahead; a fool doesn't and even brags about it!" When you're angry and want to skin someone alive—or at least flay them with a few choice words—you need to stop and consider before you act, before you speak. I think all of us know that in our unrestrained anger, we end up saying things that begin to devastate relationships and friendships more than we could imagine.

Hear me: Nothing—short of a physical blow—can kill a relationship faster than a poisonous word.

How do I deal with that anger, then? Please don't despise this simple answer: *I need to take my concerns and hurts and frustrations to the Lord.* It touches me to think that the Lord came down to talk and reason with Cain in his deadly anger. The Lord made himself available to this man. And how different it would have been if Cain had taken that walk through the orchard with the Lord and said, "You're right, Lord. I *am* down about this. I am angry. It hurts me that You'd accept Abel's offering and not accept mine, and I'm having trouble dealing with it. Could You just help me, Lord? Could You walk with me for a few minutes and help me sort things through?"

Do you know what I tell the Lord in a situation like that? I say, "God, I just need to tell You I'm going to need some help with this. In my own strength, this isn't going to go on much longer before I open my mouth and let someone know how I'm feeling."

Just tell Him. Pour it out. He can handle it. He already knows it all, and He stands ready to help.

That's precisely what the disciples needed to discover after the Lord said to them, "I don't want you to just forgive someone seven times, but seventy times seven!" At first blush, the disciples must have thought, "There's no way. It isn't going to happen. We're not going to buy into this seventy-times-seven deal." But what did they say? "Lord, if You're serious about this, then You'd better increase our faith and change our hearts…because the way we're feeling right now, there's no way we can do anything less than retaliate and let them know how angry and upset we really are." (See Matthew 18:21–22; Luke 17:3–5.)

This is the very thing that happens in the so-called "plaintive psalms." David or another psalmist begins with a complaint or an invective against someone. Go get 'em, God. Bring 'em down. Break their teeth and bring justice to them. And yet so often, he ends up having his focus changed and leaves the psalm with praise on his lips. He begins by being problem-centered and then becomes promise-centered.

He begins by saying, "I'm so sick about this, God. I'm so angry at these people. Why don't you do something!" Then by the end he's saying, "Now that I think about it, Lord, You've given me everything and done so much for me. I'm just going to think about how kind You've been to me."

Psalm 73 is a wonderful example of this. The psalmist, Asaph, launches out with a bitter complaint to the Lord. He pulls out the cork on his frustrations and lets all that anger drain out in God's presence. And then, after a while, he says this:

When I thought how to understand this,
It was too painful for me—
Until I went into the sanctuary of God;
Then I understood their end.
(Psalm 73:16–17)

Asaph took his pain and perplexity and anger into the temple. He went into the Lord's presence and spread it all out before God. And then the lights came on. As he gazed upon the Lord, his anger and all the injustice that had bothered him so deeply became a secondary issue. And how does he leave the presence of the Lord?

He ends the psalm with these choice words:

But it is good for me to draw near to God;
I have put my trust in the Lord GOD,
That I may declare all your works.
(Psalm 73:28)

What do you do with your anger? What do you do with your pain and hurt? Bring it into the Lord's presence. Bring the whole, knotted, tangled, twisted-up mass of it and lay it before Him. Let Him sort it out as you kneel in His presence. And when you leave you will find yourself saying, "This has been good. It is good for me to draw near to God. What a mighty God He is!"

❧

Lord, thank You for changing my heart. I've asked for more and more of You, and that's why I'm seeing less and less of me. Hallelujah. Once my life was filled with unforgiveness and anger, but no more. You have produced in me the spirit of love, joy, peace, long-suffering, gentleness, goodness, faith, meekness, and self-control. I don't feel the need to do Your job any more. I trust You to administer justice and bring righteousness in Your own way and in Your own time. Thank You for tempering wrath with mercy, as You did in my life, for Jesus' sake.

And so today, Lord, I will value and protect life…because You do. In Jesus' name, amen.

"You shall not commit adultery."

＊

GOD'S FENCE
AROUND
YOUR MARRIAGE

THE REASON FOR THE FENCE

When I think of the Ten Commandments, an odd picture sometimes comes to mind.

Now, you might visualize Charlton Heston standing on top
of a mountain with a dusky sky behind him, the stone tablets in
his upraised arms, and the fire of God in his eyes.

Personally, I think of a rodeo. In particular, I think of a sad
little Associated Press news item I saw recently.

SAN DIEGO: An 18-year-old bull rider who was kicked
and trampled by a 2,300-pound Brahma bull during a
Sept. 18 rodeo has died from his injuries, hospital officials said.

Paul Coronado died Tuesday at Sharp Memorial
Hospital. He had been unconscious and in critical con-
dition since being trampled during the Lakeside Rodeo.
Coronado had been competing professionally in rodeos
for only a few months since graduating from El Capitan
High School in June.

Family and friends who had maintained a bedside vigil since his injury were there when he died at 10:04 P.M., according to a family member. Services for Coronado are pending.

Have you ever watched a rider hanging for dear life on to the back of a Brahma bull? When that bull swings his massive head and shoulders and sends the rider into the air—and then into the sawdust—the cowboy's natural instincts kick in, and he begins to run. He heads toward the fence as fast as he can go, wishing—for a second or two, maybe—that it wasn't there. But then after scaling the barrier in one bound and finding it between him and two thousand pounds of raging bull, he feels pretty good about that old fence. He might even lean over and give it a kiss. He's mighty glad it's there.

In the seconds before he was trampled, young Paul Coronado must have wished fervently for a fence between him and the angry beast he'd been trying to ride. But it all happened too quickly. He didn't have a chance to get away.

Why should a rodeo cowboy love a fence? Because the fence isn't there to restrict and restrain the rider, it is there to restrain the bull. That's what God's commandments do for us; they protect us. They put a barrier between us and that which would destroy us. They place a restraint on our flesh that wants what it wants *at any cost.*

In our fallen human nature, we like to avoid "commands," don't we? We didn't like commands as children, and the truth is, we don't much like them as adults, either. Words like *can't, shouldn't,* or *must* sound harsh in our ears. We're all a bit like

Esau, willing (in our flesh) to trade *anything*—even our very birthright—for a plate of stew to satisfy our hunger of the moment. Our flesh cares nothing for happiness tomorrow or peace of heart for a lifetime. It cares nothing about the well-being of those we love. All it seeks is gratification NOW.

That's the legacy of our first parents...the long, cold shadow of Adam and Eve. If you see a sign on a door that says "Do Not Enter," what's your first inclination? Most of us want to at least take a peek inside to see what all the fuss is about.

If I see a detour sign, I'm not overly excited about taking a twenty-mile alternate route. I think to myself, "That sign probably isn't valid. I'll bet they finished the work on Friday and just haven't taken the signs down yet. I can probably get through now." Typically, I'll try. Often I'll get myself into trouble and an even *longer* delay.

In *The Magician's Nephew,* one of C. S. Lewis's Chronicles of Narnia classics, two English children, Digory and Polly, are presented with a dilemma while exploring a strange, ancient world. In the crumbling ruins of a once-great palace, they come across a beautiful golden bell, somehow untarnished by the passing ages. Lying beside the bell is a tiny golden hammer. Below the bell is a sign. At first the children can't read the letters. But as they stare at the sign, the words seem to reform themselves into English, with this warning:

> Make your choice, adventurous Stranger:
> Strike the bell and bide the danger,
> Or wonder, till it drives you mad,
> What would have followed if you had.[1]

Polly shrinks away from the bell. She wants nothing to do with the danger. She wants to go home! Digory, however, is seized with an insatiable curiosity. Before Polly can stop him, he suddenly grabs the hammer and strikes the bell. It immediately produces a clear, sweet note. But rather than fading, the sound of the bell begins to grow and grow—until it becomes deafening. Walls and buildings begin to collapse under the massive reverberation, and the children barely escape with their lives. Through a series of circumstances that follow, Digory's impulsive decision brings tragedy beyond anything he could have imagined.

People will say, "Well, I can do what I want to do. It's my life. I can live the way I want to live and go where I want to go. If there's a sign that says, 'Don't do this,' I'll do it anyway, if I can get away with it. If God says, 'Don't commit adultery,' it's really none of His business." Yet it is His world, His creation, and it is His business whether or not people obey His commands. He loves people like you and me so much that He has made a list of restrictions to protect us from that which would be so extremely destructive to our lives and the lives of those we love.

Adultery is one of those things.

As with the bell in Lewis's book, the consequences of adultery roll on and on, growing in their destructive intensity, and impacting generation after generation.

Why should God be so concerned about adultery in particular? Why should purity and faithfulness in a marriage be so very important to Him? Because He knows that the home and the church are the two institutions ordained of God on earth to visibly model the love of God. It is in Satan's interest to mar and disfigure both of those models. In particular, Satan seeks the destruction of married love and the family. How quickly we forget that "our struggle is not against flesh and blood, but against the rulers, against the authorities, against the powers of this dark world and against the spiritual forces of evil in the heavenly realms" (Ephesians 6:12, NIV).

I don't watch much TV, but I've seen enough to know that on any given evening you shouldn't be shocked to encounter a constant parade of seduction and suggestive sexual encounters. Virtually every program is riddled with immorality, seduction, and flirtation.

It's adultery, plain and simple. But Hollywood has made it all appear so romantic, exciting, fulfilling, and even funny. The image makers surround it with laughter, beautiful music, and sumptuous settings. At the same time, they carefully airbrush away the inevitable shame, deceit, betrayal, and ugliness.

People who witness these make-believe encounters begin to think, "My life is so dull. So unromantic. Where is the music? Where is the laughter? Maybe this is what I need. Maybe this will fill that gaping empty place in my heart." Those who spin these silky, perfumed myths never show you what follows in real life *after* such an "affair." They never show the bills coming due. They never show the tears. The movie versions of the David and Bathsheba story don't bother with the resulting pain, death, and devastation. David's an impressive hulk, and she's Miss Israel. It's always silk sheets and marble tubs, a palace with servants—the works. But they never tell you what happened in the remaining years of David's life and the tortured history of his shattered family.

Satan reminds me of an unprincipled used car salesman (the kind who only cares about that one sale, not a long-term relationship). He says, "What can I do to get you into this car today?" You say, "Well, it's a nice car, all right, but I need to go home and talk to my family and look at my budget." And he replies, "No, no, you need to buy this car *now*. Listen, I can make it all possible for you. If you go home it may not be here when you get back. You'll never have a deal like this again. We'll take care of you. You deserve this. You need this. Just step into this little white room and I'll get the papers ready."

Satan doesn't want us to think beyond "now." He doesn't want us to consider our actions. He doesn't want us to ponder the consequences or look down the road. He doesn't want us to think about how many payments we will be making for the rest of our lives.

I heard about a counselor who asked the question, "What effect will my actions have if I go through a door called Desire?" He decided to write them down. He said, If I go through that door…

I will grieve the One who redeemed me.

I will drag His sacred name through the mud.

I will have to look Jesus in the eye one day and give an account of my actions.

I will inflict untold hurt on my wife, who is my best friend and who has been faithful to me.

I will lose my wife's respect, love, and trust.

I will hurt my beloved daughters.

I will destroy my example and credibility.

I might lose my wife and children forever.

I will shame my family.

I will lose my own self-respect. (Though God could forgive me, could I forgive myself?)

I could form memories and flashbacks that plague future intimacy with my spouse.

I could reap the consequences of diseases.

I could cause a pregnancy that would be a lifelong reminder of my sin.

I could invoke lifelong shame and embarrassment on myself.

Wise man. He's looking at the bill and wondering what kind of a "deal" Satan is really placing before him. He's looking hard at the terms and the payment plan.

To return to an earlier picture, he is standing securely and safely behind a high, white barricade, while all hell breaks loose on the other side. And the fence that once seemed so unyielding and restrictive now seems very, very beautiful to him. It seems like life itself.

WHERE ADULTERY BEGINS

Some will say, "I've never committed adultery and never would. This is a waste of time. This isn't applicable at all to my life."

Really? Can you still say that after remembering Jesus' words in Matthew 5:27–28?

"You have heard that it was said to those of old, 'You shall not commit adultery.' But I say to you that whoever looks at a woman to lust for her has already committed adultery with her in his heart."

Back in 1975, then-presidential candidate Jimmy Carter told an interviewer that while he had never committed adultery, he knew he had failed the Lord many times by entertaining adultery in his heart. The press couldn't handle such a forthright admission. They mocked him for months; it was a big joke in the media. Looking back now, however, the man's honesty seems refreshing.

Who among us hasn't failed the Lord in this area of mental adultery? And where else does adultery begin, if not in the mind? The truth is, there is no such thing as a one-night stand. An affair begins to play itself out on the stage of imagination long before it occurs in real life.

The real battle in your life and mine is the battle of the mind. That's where it began with Eve, and it's where the battle has raged ever since. Satan begins to whisper in your ear, and you find yourself thinking about what you want, what you "deserve," what you "need," and what ("by all rights") you should have.

When God says, "Heed My Word," we need to remember that He has watched countless people walk to and fro across the surface of this planet from the very beginning. He has watched the pain and the consequences and the trouble that have come as a result of every violation of this seventh commandment. How could a loving God do less than warn us? How could He do less than set His protective fences down across the landscape of our lives and urge us to walk safely within them?

How does adultery begin to suggest itself to an unguarded heart? Let me show you some sources that have come up in my counseling with couples through the years.

Immaturity and Conflicts

Whenever you have a relationship, you have conflicts. Why should that be such a shock? We're impatient people, in our flesh. I want results now; I want this fixed now; I want this handled now. And if couples don't address those conflicts, they will find themselves becoming disillusioned and drawing apart. One dead giveaway of an immature relationship is the inability to work toward a goal out beyond the immediate. Instead, we say, I want my needs met *right now*. I'm not going to wait a week, I'm not going to wait a day, I'm not going to wait an hour.

That's nothing but immaturity.

Immaturity always says, I want what I want when I want it. Just listen to a little child when he gets hungry. He won't take no for answer. He won't be soothed by the words "a little later," or "just a minute." He's hungry, he wants his bottle, and he wants it *now*. He won't stop screaming until he gets it.

Some years ago I spoke to a man who was having an affair because, he said, he'd "finally found a woman who loves me and cares about me." This other woman was young and vivacious, someone he could really talk to. And his wife? "Well, frankly, Pastor," he said, "my wife isn't what she used to be. She's always tired."

Knowing this man and the kind of attitude he had, I felt freedom to be very frank.

"You say your wife is always tired?" I asked.

"Yeah," he said. "She never wants to do anything anymore."

"I have an opinion about that," I told him. "Let me tell you why she's always so tired. Number one, it's because she's had to serve you and put up with your ingratitude and bad temper through all these years. And number two, it's because she's had to bear, care for, and raise your children almost single-handedly, because you were never around to help. Anyone could get weary and tired with *that* kind of assignment. It makes me tired just thinking about it."

I believe the greatest contributor to divorce is not "incompatibility," but irresponsibility and immaturity. I've discovered over the years that virtually every couple goes through the same basic challenges in a marriage. But the difference between the couple that gets divorced and the one that doesn't is wrapped up in one word: commitment.

Why is commitment such a rare commodity in our world today? Because we enter into marriage looking for someone to serve us, rather than someone to serve. In a word, we are selfish.

Some say that love is based on *passion*. "I'm empty without you, but if I can have you, I'll be fulfilled and satisfied." That may be the definition some use for love, but I can promise you it's not the kind of love that will hold together and last.

Some say that love is based on *need*. "I need you and I'll never make it if I don't have you." But six months from now, you may find yourself "needing" someone else. Love that is based on need can never be satisfied, because man is built to be satisfied by only one Person, and His name is Jesus.

Biblical love is a love that is based on *commitment*. The

whole purpose of that kind of love is to serve, satisfy, and fulfill the person to whom you've committed your life.

One of the chief falsehoods in Satan's Great Encyclopedia of Lies is that love is a "feeling." No! Love is not a feeling. It may certainly produce wonderful feelings, as do many other of God's blessings in our lives. But genuine love is still love when you can no longer find the feelings. Genuine love is still love when you wake up one morning and don't feel anything at all. Love is commitment. Was it a warm, fuzzy feeling that kept Jesus on the cross? Is it a feeling that causes Him to love and forgive us when we fail? No, it is His love for us, it is His commitment to us. If love were based on feeling, how could God love me at all? Because we all stumble and fail. Yet He loves us with a committed love.

Expectations

We have expectations of people we love, but they often go unmet. We put pressure on these people to believe that somehow *they* are the ones who are going to satisfy us, fulfill us, and meet every need we have. God knows that you and I can invest in one another, love one another, and be a blessing to one another, but He is the One who is the satisfier. He is the One who fulfills in every regard.

There is no man or woman in the world who can fill all the empty places in your heart. Solomon had a thousand wives, and who knows how many concubines, yet he ended up as empty as a man can be. Only the Lord God can fill the vacuum in a human heart.

Lack of Nurture

Don't deprive your mate of the love and affection—both emotional and physical—that you promised when you stood together before the altar. Don't deprive one another, because if you do, you will become very vulnerable.

A person who commits adultery usually talks about "needing someone to love me." But what we really need in a relationship isn't to find someone who can love and fulfill us, but someone we can serve. Our greatest need in life is to serve people, and you'll never be a servant to anyone else until first you're a servant to your spouse and family.

Some time ago, I read about a man named Johnny Lingo, who lived on a Pacific island. The custom on his little island was this: when a young man found a girl he wanted to marry, he paid his future father-in-law a certain number of cows for the daughter's hand.

Now, two to three cows could buy you an average, perfectly adequate wife. Four or five cows could get you a highly satisfactory one. Johnny loved a girl named Sarita. Sarita had always been very plain. She was thin, her shoulders were hunched over, and she walked with her head ducked down. Yet Johnny paid Sarita's father eight cows. The islanders said to one another, "*Eight cows?* This is ridiculous. He got cheated." It was the talk of the community.

A visitor who had heard of the eight-cow betrothal came to Johnny's house to do some business with him. As they were talking, Sarita entered the room to set a vase of flowers on the table. And it seemed to the visitor that the flowers weren't nearly as fresh and beautiful and vibrant as the wife of Johnny Lingo. She was not at all like the Sarita he had heard about. She was one of the loveliest women he had ever seen. There was something in the lift of her shoulders, the tilt of her chin, and the sparkle of her eyes.

Johnny noticed his guest's wide-eyed response to his wife. When Sarita had left the room, Johnny said to his guest, "Have you ever thought about what it must mean to a woman to know that her husband had settled on the lowest price for which she could be bought? Did you ever wonder what it must feel like to her, when the women talk and boast of what their husbands paid for them? One says, 'Four cows,' another 'five cows,' or maybe even 'six cows.' How does she feel, the woman who was sold for one or two?

"I decided this must not happen to my Sarita," said Johnny. "I wanted to marry Sarita. I loved her and no other woman. I wanted Sarita to be happy…but I wanted even more than that. I wanted her and everyone else to know that she is worth more than any other woman to me."

What a wise man. Because of his love, she became the most beautiful woman on the island. Maintaining a healthy love relationship does take a bit of work, but oh, friend, it is worth it a thousand times over. The Scriptures say to submit to one another. When you love and care for someone, you build in that person the capacity to do the same! He or she gets to love you, think of you, pamper you, and put you first, too.

The Lord has made a commitment to you and me as well. He has chosen us and purchased us, and it wasn't with cows. It was a payment beyond price or comprehension.

For you know that it was not with perishable things such as silver or gold that you were redeemed from the empty way of life handed down to you from your forefathers, but with the precious blood of Christ, a lamb without blemish or defect. (1 Peter 1:18–19, NIV)

Why is it that my life has been totally turned around? It's because when I came to Jesus I discovered what He did to draw me close, to bring me close to Himself. And now I know I am loved by Him. That's why His ongoing commitment to me has made me realize how important it is that I have an ongoing commitment to those that I love. To Joyce. To the boys. It's not *their* jobs to convince themselves that I love them. It's my job to convince them. It's not my job to convince myself that God loves me; that's God's job. That's what the Holy Spirit—the Spirit of adoption—does. He's constantly reminding us, "Remember, I love you. I bought you. I purchased you. You're mine."

I don't know why it is, but in the dating season, couples are always looking their best. They look good. They smell good. They remember the little things. They lie awake at night trying to think of ways to honor and please one another. Then, when they get married, something begins to change. It isn't as important anymore. That's one of the reasons people become vulnerable. They feel devalued.

It makes me think back to Grandpa and Grandma Simmonds, who used to be part of our fellowship before they went to be with the Lord. Richard Simmonds was ninety-four, and a very funny, sweet man. His wife's name was Caroline.

As Joyce and I would sit with the couple in their tiny living room, Richard would look out the window and say, "Well, it sure is a cloudy, dreary day today." Inevitably, Caroline would turn to him and tenderly say, "Yes, it is, but tomorrow is going to be sunny and warm."

I remember the time Joyce and I were sitting at the dining room table with Richard while Caroline was working on a little lunch for us, getting things out of the cupboard. I was talking to Richard, but he wasn't paying any attention to me. His eyes were fixed on Caroline, working in the kitchen. He was really zoned out and had no idea what I was saying to him. Finally he turned to Joyce with a smile and said, "Isn't she wonderful? Isn't she *wonderful?*"

I couldn't believe it! Here was a man pushing one hundred, and he looked like some kid on his first date. Here was a couple who had continued to cultivate and nurture their love for one another through all of their lives. And, by the way, think of what both of them would have been missing in their old age had one of them broken up the relationship through a careless act of adultery.

Grandpa Simmonds stayed behind the fence.

Grandpa Simmonds was a happy man.

WHAT IF I'VE ALREADY FAILED?

I think I could safely say that we have *all* failed in this command. Is there anyone who has never allowed an impure, adulterous thought to linger on the screen of the mind? And the Lord tells us that if we have committed adultery in our mind, it is the same in heaven's eyes as if we'd already followed through on the act.

So what can we do?

Make a Decision to Repent and Confess Your Sin to the Lord

To confess is simply to agree with God that He is right in what He says about our sin. To repent means to change course; you're headed in one direction, and you stop and turn in a different direction. You say to the Lord, "Lord, I turn from this right now—while it's still just something in my mind and my emotions. By the power of Your Spirit within me, I put these thoughts to death."

The Lord says that when we confess our sins He is faithful and just to forgive our sins and to cleanse us from all unrighteousness (1 John 1:9).

Accept His Forgiveness

Even after we have confessed and repented of our sin, our emotions may refuse to come along for a while. Some people will say, "I still feel dirty—like there's something wrong and I'm not clean."

I remember when I was a kid taking a bath, I liked to lie down so that the water covered my neck and came up into my ears. I submerged! I liked to lie there and relax in that warm, sudsy water. That's what the Lord wants to do with us. He wants to cover us with His blood and wash us clean, white as snow.

> Let us draw near with a true heart in full assurance of faith, having our hearts sprinkled from an evil conscience and our bodies washed with pure water. (Hebrews 10:22)

End the Relationship Now

Right now. Not tomorrow. Not a week from now. There is no easy way out, and yes, someone is always going to get hurt. But the only way to end it is to END it. No more conversations, no more phone calls, no more meetings. None. It's over. "Missionary dating" is a farce. Don't tell yourself, "I'll change him," or "I'll save her." I'm sorry, but if God hasn't touched that individual's life in the last five or six months—or years—what makes you think *you* are going to do it? Make the decision right now. "Lord, thank You for changing me and cleansing me. This thing is over."

Thank God

Thank Him for His restoration and resurrection power. Some people need restoration because things in their lives and marriages are broken and need to be fixed. Others need resurrection because something has died and cannot live again apart from the touch of the One who is Life.

Praise God for His mercy! Remember the woman in Scripture who was caught in adultery? They hauled her in front of all those heavy-duty teachers and theologians and made her stand there in her shame and her terror. As you read the account in John, it's obvious that they had arranged the whole episode to trap her and catch her. And now when she looked around the circle of men, she saw death in every set of eyes…save one. What did the Lord say to these men?

"Who of you is without sin? Who of you has never done this or thought it in your secret heart? Let that one cast the first stone."

And one by one, the rocks began to fall out of hands that were no longer so eager to hurl them. And one by one, the would-be accusers walked away.

> And Jesus was left alone, and the woman standing in the midst. When Jesus had raised Himself up and saw no one but the woman, He said to her, "Woman, where are those accusers of yours? Has no one condemned you?" She said, "No one, Lord." And Jesus said to her, "Neither do I condemn you; go and sin no more." (John 8:9–11)

Was He excusing sin? No. He was forgiving it. And He has perfect right and authority to do just that.

I'm not suggesting in this chapter that your marriage will never run into problems or have to endure storms. God doesn't have in mind that marriage—or any human relationship—will be problem free. Yet I believe the kind of commitment God is talking about means that when you hit a snag or difficulty in your marriage, that you make a decision to get up, dust your-selves off, and carry on together.

I love the story of Walter Peyton, the greathearted, Hall of Fame running back for the Chicago Bears. Greatly esteemed and highly regarded, Peyton's rushing yards are unparalleled. But what amazes me most about this man was his commitment. Through his long career, he rushed more than *nine miles* with a football.

Not long ago, two television football commentators were talking about Peyton's accomplishments. One said, "Can you believe that Walter Peyton has run more than nine miles with the football?" The other announcer replied, "Let me tell you what's really amazing. Did you know that every 3.8 yards Peyton was knocked down by a guy twice his size? And he did *that* for nine miles."

Every 3.8 yards, the man got hit by what seemed to be a freight train. But do you know what he did? He got back up, tucked in his shirt, and trotted (or limped) back to the huddle. It was Walter Peyton's commitment that kept him going through all those miles of bruising hits and hard knocks.

That principle works just the same in a marriage. And the best part is this: when you have the Lord in your life, He's blocking for you! You don't have to keep that commitment alone.

Lord, You are the faithful one. You are faithful in Your every thought, Your every word, Your every action. You have promised You would never leave me nor forsake me, and You have proven that commitment over and over again. You've stayed at my side through good times and dark times, in sickness and in health. You've promised that if I fail, You'll still love me. You are so good, so ready to forgive, so abundant in mercy. Your unconditional love has redeemed me, healed me, and freed me. Day by day, You are shaping me into Your own image, bringing forth beauty where it never was before.

And so, today, Lord, help me to be faithful to my life partner—this wonderful person You have given me to love—in every word, every thought, every deed. In Jesus' name, amen.

"You shall not steal."

EXODUS 20:15

❦

LETTING GOD
MEET YOUR NEEDS

Stealing may take place on a large scale or a very small one. Does the Lord condemn the one and wink at the other?

At one end of the scale, you have unprincipled men like Charles Keating, who wiped out the savings of thousands of investors in a multimillion dollar savings and loan swindle.

At the other end, you have Ron Mehl and a candy machine.

I was attending a convention in another state years ago, staying in a hotel, and probably feeling lonely and sorry for myself. Restless, I got up in the night and walked down the hall to find a vending machine. If I couldn't be with Joyce, I could at least buy a Snickers bar. Small comfort, but better than nothing!

I dropped my coins into the first machine I found, pushed the appropriate button, and waited for my candy. But nothing came out. No candy. No coins. Great, I thought, just great. Frustrated, I hauled off and hit the machine. Immediately, ten Snickers bars dropped out, along with my coins.

When I saw all that loot, I thought, "Oh boy, God really does provide!" This was like the Genesis story of Benjamin getting a sackful of grain and his silver back besides. Being a spiritual young man, I reasoned, "I can tithe this. Maybe that's why God showered me with Snickers." I would set aside one candy bar for the Lord and eat the other nine.

I took my stash back to the room and ate one of the "free" bars.

It was a funny thing. Snickers has always been my favorite candy bar...but this one didn't taste very good. I ate it kind of fast. It stuck in my throat just a little. I began to feel guilty about eating something I hadn't paid for. To console myself, I ate another one. By the time I'd finished that second Snickers, I didn't feel consoled at all. I felt like a crook. I couldn't even sleep that night (I don't know if it was the candy bars or the conviction).

The next morning I confessed all to the Lord and to the manager at the front desk.

The Lord heard me right away, but the manager was busy with several other things and didn't really want to be bothered with my conscience and candy bars. It was a hassle for him. He'd have to tell the candy machine guy and keep the Snickers bars lying around.

"Come on," he said. "You've got to be kidding. Just take the candy you have left and forget it. Call it your lucky day."

Not a chance. That manager was either going to deal with my stolen loot or have me stand there all day looking at him. When I finally got it all settled, I knew that I could go and enjoy my breakfast. The bacon and eggs were going to slide down nice and easy. They weren't going to stick in my throat.

I wonder how Charles Keating enjoyed his breakfasts. I remember watching television news coverage on the savings-and-loan swindler, booked on federal charges of racketeering, conspiracy, and fraud. He was sentenced to twelve years and seven months in prison (but was recently set free on a legal technicality).

This was a man who had siphoned millions of dollars from Lincoln Savings and Loan in Irvine, California, into high-risk financial schemes that went bust. Mostly retired investors lost more than 285 million dollars—their life savings wiped out in an instant.

Do you remember watching his sentencing on television? It was depressing. Before the court passed sentence, the defense team brought in Keating's children and grandchildren. They wept before the judge, saying, "Please don't sentence our father and grandfather like this. We love our grandpa. He's a good man. But if he goes to prison, he'll die there, and we won't get to grow up with him or spend time with him. Please don't do this to him."

Do you think Mr. Keating ever thought for a moment about those consequences to his actions? Did the candy he bought with all that money ever stick in his throat? Did he ever visualize or imagine such a tearful courtroom scene? Did he think about the distress of his children and grandchildren? Was he deceived…or just prideful and arrogant?

The eighth commandment basically speaks to taking something that doesn't belong to me. And yes, it applies equally to the assets of a savings and loan and a vending machine Snickers bar. Amazingly, we use more than a hundred synonyms to describe the act of stealing. People steal, thieve, purloin, snatch, palm, bag, filch, cop, pinch…take your pick. I guess that means we've learned how to do it in a whole lot of ways—some big, some not so big. Some subtle, some not so subtle.

How do people end up stealing? Some do it knowingly. They borrow money from someone knowing very well they'll never pay it back. Some people steal in even more subtle ways—perhaps robbing from their employers by habitually taking long lunch breaks. I tease Joyce about doing that in her work here at the church. But then again, we don't pay her anything, so I guess we can't complain too much. All she has to do is smile sweetly at us and say, "Go ahead and make my day...fire me!"

But why would the Lord make "Do not steal" one of the Ten? Why is this so important to His heart that He would include it with restrictions against murder, adultery, and worshiping false gods?

As I pondered that question, I actually went to the Lord to ask Him about it. "Lord," I prayed, "I believe every one of these commands pertains to Your love for me. They are *tender* commandments. But how does this one fit? How does this eighth command demonstrate Your love?"

The answer, when it hit me, seemed all too obvious.

What God must be saying is this: "I don't want you stealing because I am your Provider. I want you to understand and believe that I am the One who will supply all your needs. I don't want you to have to scheme, manipulate, and deceive to obtain things. For then what would you become? A schemer, a manipulator, and a deceiver. I don't want you to feel responsible for securing your own future."

The truth is, every time we steal something—whether large or small—we are saying, "I will be my own provider in this instance. If I don't take it now, I will be the loser."

But the Lord wants us to understand that when we place our

trust fully in Him, we are *never* the loser. Through this commandment, the Lord wanted to say to the people of Israel—and to us as well—Let Me provide for you. I want you to trust Me, rest in Me, and be contented with Me."

The Lord has given us, as Peter says, great and precious promises. He has pledged Himself to satisfy and supply our every need.

Why do people steal? Scripture give us several insights.

Because They Want Instant Happiness

God understands this motivation, as He understands all of Satan's traps. The Deceiver convinces me that taking something now will give me an immediate lift. It will fill a void in my life and ease that empty discontentment I feel (which can only be filled by the Lord Himself).

In His tenderness, God wants to spare us from the humiliation and damage stealing can do to our family and to the people we love. In His mercy, He wants to shield us from the curse this activity brings upon our lives.

If you don't believe stealing is costly, ask Achan in the book of Joshua.

The Lord had told Joshua and the people of Israel that all of the goods from the conquered city of Jericho were to be devoted to Him. Anything of value was to go into the Lord's treasury. Those were the conditions of the military operation, and there could be no misunderstanding God's clear instructions:

> "The city and all that is in it are to be devoted to the
> LORD.... Keep away from the devoted things, so that you

will not bring about your own destruction by taking any of them. Otherwise you will make the camp of Israel liable to destruction and bring trouble on it." (Joshua 6:17, 18, NIV)

And trouble is exactly what came when Achan deliberately violated that clear command. What did he do? Hear it from his own lips:

"This is what I have done: When I saw in the plunder a beautiful robe from Babylonia, two hundred shekels of silver and a wedge of gold weighing fifty shekels, I coveted and took them. They are hidden in the ground inside my tent." (Joshua 7:20–21, NIV)

Rather than waiting on God to supply what he desired, Achan took what did not belong to him, and it brought a stinging defeat to the army of Israel. Instead of marching across the Promised Land in a great victory tour, the Lord's army stumbled. And they stumbled over the sin of one man.

It also brought a death sentence to Achan and his family. When the Israelites walked away from the pile of rocks that became the family's grave, they named the place the Valley of Achor, or the *Valley of Trouble.*

All this for one act of stealing!

What Achan didn't know was that, just a few days later, God would have provided him with more than his meager haul at Jericho. In the very next battle, God permitted all of the plunder to go to the troops. All of it. Within hours, had he only waited, had he only obeyed and trusted, Achan's family might have been blessed immeasurably. Achan might have had a far better cloak than that red Babylonian garment that had caught his eye. He might have had more silver and gold than what he took by deception and hid under his tent.

This whole account seems to speak about trusting God's timing and provision. Not running ahead of Him to provide for our own needs. Not running ahead of Him to grab our own happiness or comfort or security. He wants us to wait for Him, and to wait for His timing. Even if we have to wait through the very few years of our lives to enjoy the unimaginable splendor in heaven, *it is better to wait!*

Peter says,

> Praise be to the God and Father of our Lord Jesus Christ! In his great mercy he has given us new birth...into an inheritance that can never perish, spoil or fade—kept in heaven for you, who through faith are shielded by God's power. (1 Peter 1:3–5, NIV)

What are the few piddly trinkets and toys of this earth compared to the splendor and beauty of riches stored up for us in God's own house? Someday, when we're walking down some winding, golden path through heavenly hills, we will laugh—or perhaps weep—to realize how absorbed and preoccupied we were with trivial material things during our brief stay on earth.

God knows very well that money will not purchase happiness in this life. *He knows it!* Nor can possessions purchase peace. They never have, and they never will. Yet Satan continues to deceive us. Satan continues to tell us, "Better grab what you can now. Better take what you can get, even if it means cutting a few corners. Better stuff your pockets full. You may never have another opportunity!"

Proverbs 15:16 says, "Better is a little with the fear of the LORD, than great treasure with trouble."

Is that right, Charles Keating? Wouldn't it have been better to live in a three-bedroom apartment, wear a Wal-Mart suit, and drive a used Chevy—and enjoy the respect and admiration of your peers, your children, your grandchildren, and your God? Wouldn't it have been better than being disgraced before a whole nation and spending your declining days in prison?

Is that right, Achan? Wouldn't it have been better to wear the old homespun cloak you carried with you through the wilderness? Wouldn't it have been better to endure a thin wallet and tight finances—yet live with your wife and your strong sons and your beautiful daughters to see God's people march triumphantly across a new land flowing with milk and honey? Wouldn't it have been better than ending it all under a cold pile of rocks in the Valley of Trouble?

Isn't God's provision today, however modest it may seem, better than trying to grab for ourselves and make our own way in this brief lifetime of ours?

Your translation of Proverbs 15:17 may read something like this: "Better is a dish of vegetables where love is, than a fattened ox and hatred with it" (NASB). But my mom always quoted it to me as: "Better is a dinner of spinach and asparagus..." It took me years to discover she was messing with the text. Anything to get that green stuff down me!

But Mom and Solomon were right. It *is* better to have a dinner of veggies—even spinach—in a home where there's love and peace than to have a freezer full of beef with fear and hostility around the table. Hey, vegetables slide down just fine when there's laughter and love all around.

In 1 Timothy 6:10, Paul tells his young friend that the love of money is the root of all evil. To me, that verse is saying that the love of money is at the root of every evil, every war, every difficulty, every heartache in this big wide world of ours. So why should I have a love affair with it?

I shouldn't. I should reserve my love for Him.

Yes, we all have our work to do. And yes, we need to be responsible, make a living, and pursue excellence. But always remember it is God who provides for you. He'll provide for your future. He'll do what He said He would do. Trust Him now to do those things.

Because They Want Security

People find their security in amazing ways. I heard of one man who literally filled his garage—floor to ceiling—with Styrofoam ice chests stuffed with rolls of toilet paper. He figured, I suppose, that in a world crisis, those would be the things you'd need most.

People sometimes think, *If I can just take this and grab that, it will give me the sense of security I'm longing for.* They think security in riches and "things" will make them happy. Here is what Solomon said about that: "Do not wear yourself out to get rich; have the wisdom to show restraint. Cast but a glance at riches, and they are gone, for they will surely sprout wings and fly off to the sky like an eagle" (Proverbs 23:4–5, NIV).

Money and possessions are no security at all! I believe the Lord is saying, "Remember this...all the money that you possess and embrace by deception will fly away."

Has that ever happened to you? You look at your bank account statement or your check register and say, "What happened? I was sure I had more money than that! Where did it all go? It seemed that just yesterday we had this much, and now we don't have anything at all!"

God knows that the very things you thought were going to secure your life and future will fall short. A lingering illness can neatly erase a life's savings. A house full of possessions can be wiped out by a flood—or swept away by an unfavorable IRS audit.

The only thing secure in this life is the Lord God. As David said, "I have set the LORD always before me. Because he is at my right hand, I will not be shaken. Therefore my heart is glad" (Psalm 16:8–9, NIV).

Because They Want to Attract Friends

Some people actually believe that if you flash around a bunch of money you will get a lot of dates or attract a lot of friends. Ah, but what sort of dates? What kind of "friends"? What do the Scriptures say?

> Wealth brings many friends,
> but a poor man's friend deserts him.
> (Proverbs 19:4, NIV)

Where you have "things," you have a lot of friends—bosom pals who suddenly come out of the woodwork. If you come into an inheritance or win the Reader's Digest Sweepstakes, you'll have any number of people trying to convince you of their loyal and undying esteem.

Do you want to ask Mike Tyson whether or not he believes Proverbs 19:4? When you're winning and the money is rolling in, everybody likes you. But when you start to lose, make a few mistakes, and the money dries up, there's a stampede for the back door. The consultants are gone, the managers are gone, the sports psychologists are gone, the groupies are gone. Everyone is gone. Why? There's no money left. And that was the only reason they were there.

That sort of friend is no friend at all.

I'm so glad Joyce didn't marry me for my money. It's nice to know for sure in my heart that this beautiful woman wasn't attracted to me because of my bank account or stock portfolio. (It might have been for my brand-new, green VW Bug, but it wasn't for my money.) If she even imagined that I had a stash tucked away somewhere, the first three years of our marriage would have cured her of that impression.

Our first apartment was in a low-income housing project. We slept on the floor on a twin mattress we'd shoved up against the wall. The bedroom was just about big enough to walk around that little mattress. To flush the toilet, you had to hit the wall. Don't ask me why, but that's the way it worked. You pushed the flusher, hit the wall, and *boom,* plumbing success. It's something you got used to after a while. I still find myself wanting to bang on the bathroom wall now and then, just for old time's sake.

No, there weren't many fattened oxen on the dinner table at

night, and there might have been a few more vegetables than I'd been used to. But Mom was right. There was love around that little table. There was love in that little apartment. And there was laughter, too. The Lord provided for us in beautiful ways. They were great years, and we wouldn't trade them for a million-dollar lottery ticket—or a red Babylonian cloak, for that matter.

Because We've Forgotten About God's Promise of Care

Do you know what Joyce and I sensed the Lord telling us in those early years? It's the same thing He tells us today: "I want to provide for you. I love you. Work hard, meet your obligations, and do everything you need to do, but please remember that your future rests in My care and provisions for you."

Isn't that the message of God's Son? Please read the next paragraph very carefully.

"Therefore I say to you, do not worry about your life, what you will eat or what you will drink; nor about your body, what you will put on. Is not life more than food and the body more than clothing?

"Look at the birds of the air, for they neither sow nor reap nor gather into barns; yet your heavenly Father feeds them. Are you not of more value than they?

"Which of you by worrying can add one cubit to his stature?

"So why do you worry about clothing? Consider the lilies of the field, how they grow: they neither toil nor spin; and yet I say to you that even Solomon in all his glory was not arrayed like one of these.

"Now if God so clothes the grass of the field, which today is, and tomorrow is thrown into the oven, will He not much more clothe you, O you of little faith?

"Therefore do not worry, saying, 'What shall we eat?' or 'What shall we drink?' or 'What shall we wear?'

"For after all these things the Gentiles seek. For your heavenly Father knows that you need all these things.

"But seek first the kingdom of God and His right-eousness, and all these things shall be added to you." (Matthew 6:25–33)

The reason people steal is because they've forgotten about God. The reason people deceive, manipulate, and cut ethical corners is because they believe their future lies in their own hands. When people forget who God is, they end up being very possessive and greedy. Rather than trusting God with the blessings they have, they begin to horde and protect and guard those things.

But when you know that God is your Provider, it changes everything. It changes your heart. It changes the way you live. And it certainly changes the way you view your possessions.

I can remember picking up my first paycheck as a kid. I used to roll sod in Bloomington, Minnesota. It was tough, dirty work, and I got a cent and a half per roll. I can remember rolling the sod on that first day and bringing home a check for $5.00.

When I walked in the front door, I proudly showed the check to my mom. I was so thrilled and excited. *Five bucks!* My very first paycheck.

But the first words out of my mom's mouth were, "Part of that is the Lord's, you know."

I was taken aback, and I gripped my check even tighter. "What do you mean?" I said. "*He* didn't do any work! *He* didn't get hot and sweaty and itchy arms from rolling all that sod. I did all the rolling. He didn't roll or stack anything!" I was incensed to think I had to give up some of my paycheck.

But Mom wanted me to understand something from the very beginning. She wanted me to grasp something bigger than any paycheck I would ever receive.

"You know, son," she said quietly, "no matter how much you have or how much you make, it is God who is your Provider. Part of this money that you've earned is for the Lord, and you should pay a tithe."

I cooled down a little. In my heart, I knew she was right. "Well," I said, "how much is that?"

"Fifty cents," she replied.

I can still remember setting that money aside, because she said it was something I needed to do *first*. And I did. I spent the $4.50 and held the fifty cents for a long time. I knew it was God's but…well, I thought I'd just hold it for Him for a while. Then one Sunday I put it in the plate. As it turns out, I was glad I did, because my mom asked me that day, "Where is that fifty cents?" I think she wondered if I had gone to the big store next to the church and bought something.

"No, Mom," I told her. "I put it into the offering today." A big smile came over her face. I'll never forget that look. She was so proud.

When you seek to be rich—whether through honest means

or by dishonest schemes—the money will fly away and you'll wonder what happened. Mom always taught me that you'll be able to do a lot more with the 90 percent of what you have than if you withheld from the Lord and tried to spend the 100 percent.

The reason people steal is because they've forgotten about God. He isn't even part of the equation in their lives. Whatever they believe or say they believe, they are practical atheists, living as though He did not exist.

Trust in God and Be Satisfied

The only way you can keep this commandment is to make a decision to be satisfied. The book of Hebrews says this very pointedly:

> Let your character be free from the love of money, being content with what you have; for He Himself has said, "I will never desert you, nor will I ever forsake you," so that we confidently say, "The Lord is my helper, I will not be afraid. What shall man do to me?" (Hebrews 13:5–6, NASB)

The world will find every way it can to charge you more and give you less. There will be fewer crackers in the box, fewer potato chips in the bag, less meat in the hamburger, and fewer miles in that new car—even though it will cost you more and more every year.

But the Lord says to us, "Don't you worry about that. And don't steal or spend all of your energy trying to scheme and manipulate things to your own advantage. Because if you obey

My Word, I'll provide for your every need all the days of your life."

There are no shortages in heaven. The warehouses of heaven are filled to overflowing, and if God ever was out of stock on an item (ridiculous thought!), it would be no problem; He can make it special order, just for you.

Achan could have learned that lesson in a way he would have never forgotten. He could have deposited those trinkets into the Lord's treasury and then laughed out loud to see God's greater provision just a few days later. It could have been a story told and retold around a thousand campfires in the Promised Land. But when he tried to take a shortcut across God's commands, he ended his life in the Valley of Trouble.

It's too late for Achan, but there's still time for me and thee.

Lord, You said, "Fear not, little flock, for it is in the Father's good pleasure to give you the kingdom." Lord, everything I have is a gift from Your hand. You have truly provided all that I need. When I fret over things I want but cannot possess, I know that I am doubting Your promises. Stealing is something people do who don't know You or trust You. I know, Lord, that this world is not about the survival of the fittest or who ends up with the most toys. It's about trusting Your lovingkindness.

And so today, Lord, because You have given me everything I need for life and godliness, I will not take anything unless it is from Your hand. In Jesus' name, amen.

"You shall not bear false witness against your neighbor."

EXODUS 20:16

༄༅༅

CHAPTER 10

WORDS THAT WOUND, WORDS THAT HEAL

A middle-aged pastor in a small farming community in the Midwest had been falsely accused. It was a vicious, scandalous story, and it swept through town like a prairie fire.

"Have you heard about the pastor?"

"Can you believe it?"

"He oughta leave town."

"You'd never think such a thing to look at him, would you?"

"Guess he had a lot of us fooled."

"His poor wife."

After a period of time, however, the rumor was found to be just that…an ugly, empty rumor, without any basis in fact. But the damage had already been done. Many people in the town had believed every word and were now reluctant to revise their opinions. ("There must have been *some* truth in it, or why would everybody be talking about it?")

Some time later, the couple who had spread the false tale came under conviction of sin and went to the pastor to apologize. Confessing they had known the rumor to be false all along, they asked the offended man for forgiveness.

"Of course I will forgive you," he replied gravely. "But could I ask you to do something for me? Something that might seem rather strange at first?"

Relieved that the pastor was willing to forgive, the couple readily agreed to do whatever he asked.

"All right," he said, "here is my request. I would like you to go home and butcher one of your chickens, pluck out all of its feathers, and put the feathers in a bag. Could you do that for me?"

They nodded yes; they could certainly do that. But it seemed so strange. *Was the man asking for a chicken?*

"Next," the pastor went on, "I'd like you to go throughout the town, and at each corner, scatter some of the feathers—just a few—from the bag. Then, please take the remaining feathers and climb to the top of the old city water tower—you know, the one by the feed store—and scatter those to the wind. Could you do those things?"

They were mystified by this point but nodded in the affirmative once again.

"Fine," the pastor said, "just fine." The couple stood up to leave. But as they reached the door, he suddenly called them back. "Oh. There's just one more thing, please. After you've finished scattering all the feathers, I'd just like you to go back through town and gather them all up again. Okay? Make sure that you pick up every one you've dropped and every one you've scattered to the winds, and put them all back in the bag. Please be careful that none of the feathers is missing, and bring the bag back to me. Could you do *that* for me?"

The couple just looked at him. "Pastor, that's impossible,"

the man said. "The wind will have blown them all over three counties by then."

The pastor didn't say a word, and slowly...the truth of his word picture began to dawn on the couple, and they hung their heads. Yes, they could be forgiven for their actions, but no one could undo the damage they had done by scattering their false and slanderous words.

Why would God include this command, "You shall not bear false witness against your neighbor," as one of the Ten? What does this command have to do with God's love for us? It amazes me to realize that out of ten commandments, three concern the use of our tongue: taking His name in vain, killing by the words we speak, and now by bearing false witness.

For the Lord to say, "Be very, very careful what you say about people," illustrates how well our God knows us. He knows the danger and potential for harm in an undisciplined tongue. He knows the unspeakable damage it can do. As Solomon noted, "Death and life are in the power of the tongue" (Proverbs 18:21).

Words That Shape Lives

We damage, damn, and destroy people when we speak untrue words about them. Jesus Himself felt the sting and injustice of such treatment. In Matthew 26:59–63, the religious leaders of the day looked for false evidence to use against Him. They searched for something—anything—that could undercut His reputation. Why? Because He had the esteem and attention of the public—something they fiercely coveted. So they looked to destroy Him any way they could, knowing that words were every bit as destructive as sharp stones.

But I believe "bearing false witness" goes well beyond bringing faulty evidence into a judicial setting. As with the other commands, the Lord intended this to apply to a wide spectrum of everyday life settings.

Words are unbelievably powerful in their impact upon human life. Let me illustrate. A man comes into my office and tells me, "I just don't love my wife anymore. She's not the same person I married." And I typically reply, "If that is true, if this woman is less lovely to you today than when you were married, if she has changed in a negative way, then you have only to look as far as the words you've spoken to her in private."

A husband's words have the power to virtually shape the life of his wife. A wife's words have the power to shape the life of her husband. A parent's words have the awesome capacity to shape the life of his or her child. Do we truly believe the Word of God in this matter? Sometimes I want to shout it out loud on a rooftop: *Life and death are in the power of the tongue!* What you say (and what you do not say) and how you say something (and how you neglect to say something) will either build an individual up or—board by board, nail by nail—tear that individual down into a pile of rubble.

"Is that bearing false witness?" you ask. It certainly is. When we are not walking in the power of God's Spirit, false, damaging, crippling words will flow right out of our old fleshly nature— words that we cannot call back, no matter how we long to do so. Whenever you say something to an individual or about an individual that is less than what God would say to that individual, you are bearing false witness. And God takes such matters very, very seriously.

What *does* He want us to say to others? He is very specific about that.

> Therefore each of you must put off falsehood and speak truthfully to his neighbor, for we are all members of one body.... Do not let any unwholesome talk come out of your mouths, but only what is helpful for building others up according to their needs, that it may benefit those who listen. And do not grieve the Holy Spirit of God. (Ephesians 4:25, 29–30, NIV)

What kind of words ought we to speak? Building words. Benefiting words. Helpful words. Uplifting words. But when we utter false, demeaning, bitter words to one another, it grieves the Holy Spirit. Think of it! Our reckless words actually bring a pang of pain to the heart of God. Why? Because our Creator knows how vulnerable we are. He knows how frightfully we damage one another with our careless use of the tongue.

If you don't believe it, read James 3:8, NIV.

> No man can tame the tongue. It is a restless evil, full of deadly poison.

What does poison do? Poison sickens and kills. And it doesn't take very much! Nor does it take much poison from the tongue to sicken a relationship, alienate a loved one, or destroy a friendship of many years.

As if that weren't enough warning, James also tells us that the tongue is like a fire. It has such destructive capacity that the

Lord warns us to guard it day and night.

A friend of mine found out (after the fact) that he and his family had been living next door to an arsonist for a couple of years. The young man would deliberately set terrible forest fires, then come home in the evening, lunch pail under his arm, wave at his neighbors, thumb through his mail, and walk into the house as though nothing had happened. The fires were horribly destructive, burning beautiful stands of timber, parkland, and even luxury homes. He was eventually caught, convicted, and jailed, but the thought of having lived next door to such a person gave my friend a funny feeling.

Imagine, living next door to an arsonist! Yet the truth is, many of us do live next door to arsonists. Or maybe…we are the arsonists. James writes:

> A whole forest can be set ablaze by a tiny spark of fire, and the tongue is as dangerous as any fire, with vast potentialities for evil. It can poison the whole body; it can make the whole of life a blazing hell. (James 3:5–6, Phillips)

There are those who start terrible, raging fires with their words. It may be only a tiny spark, here and there—something no bigger than a single match. But what can one match do? It can destroy a city. It can wipe away the work of generations. It can devastate ten thousand lives. Then these same people who have started raging fires with their words come home at night, wave at their neighbors, thumb through their mail, and walk into their homes as though nothing had happened. You would never believe the damage and devastation they have just produced.

God intended our words to bring counsel and encouragement and blessing. *My words were meant to deliver healing and sustenance and sweetness and seasoning—not killing poison.* Proverbs 16:24 (NIV) says, "Pleasant words are a honeycomb, sweet to the soul and healing to the bones."

A Witness to the World

God intends that the words of His church would touch the world. And when we speak lovingly and respectfully to one another, then, as He has told us, "By this shall all men know that you are My disciples, because you have love one for another." God knew that loving words—matched with loving deeds!—would be the greatest source of evangelism.

Paul wrote: "Live wisely among those who are not Christians, and make the most of every opportunity. Let your conversation be gracious and effective so that you will have the right answer for everyone" (Colossians 4:5–6, NLT).

But what if I am one of those who has dropped matches in the wrong places? What if I have spread cynical poison or toxic criticism? What can I do? How can I get my tongue back under control?

Realize Only God Can Change the Way You Speak

You can go to any seminar, listen to any tape, or read any book about seven ways to speak positive, wonderful words. But when you're all done, you're probably not going to be capable of doing those seven things. And neither am I. I will do them for two or three days, perhaps, but then in an unguarded moment I'll turn around and just bludgeon somebody with angry words, or poison the waters with an oil slick of sarcasm. I'll follow those self-improvement plans for a while, and then I will revert to form. I will say something I should never have said and long to call the words back.

Every now and then you read a horrible story in the news of a child mauled by some wild animal that had supposedly been domesticated. "It was tame!" the keepers protest. "It was trained. It was safe. It had never hurt anyone else." But somehow, this "tamed" cougar, leopard, or wolf will suddenly revert back to an old instinct—to attack, to lash out, to maim and kill. Our tongue has that same awful potential. Just when we think we've got our mouths under control, just when we think our tongue has been tamed and gentled and civilized, something will set us off and we will *maul* someone with our angry or bitter words.

Our tongue is like a wild animal, and James said that no man can tame it. There's a simple reason for that. *It is because only God can.*

You'll never be able to train your tongue to bring life instead of death. Real healing comes in your heart and mind when you realize that only God can accomplish these things in your life. He is the only one who can turn bitter water sweet. The people of Israel learned that lesson just a short time before they received the Ten Commandments. They came to a place called Marah, and found the water there too bitter to drink. And what happened? *They* became bitter.

And the people murmured against Moses, saying, "What shall we drink?"

So he cried out to the LORD, and the LORD showed him a tree; and when he cast it into the waters, the waters were made sweet. (Exodus 15:24–25)

God is in the business of turning the bitter water sweet in our lives. You and I can't do it. We can add food coloring or sugar or flavoring to try to disguise the bitter taste, but we cannot make it pure and sweet. He can. Because Jesus tasted the bitterness of suffering and death for us, we can experience life that is as pure and sweet and clear as an artesian spring. God showed Moses a tree in that place of bitterness, and He shows us a tree as well, in the midst of our bitterness…the cross of our Lord Jesus.

Respond to the Holy Spirit's Promptings

Have you ever wanted to tell someone something—yet knew you really shouldn't?

I was speaking to a woman on our staff recently and said, "You know, I probably shouldn't tell you this…" I guess I was hoping she'd respond, "Oh come on…go ahead! Let's hear it! It's probably not that big of a deal."

Instead she looked at me and said, "Well then, I guess you'd better not."

That set me back on my heels for a moment. I wasn't expecting that response! I smiled, kept my lip buttoned, and walked away. I already respected that lady a great deal, and now I respect her even more. The Spirit of God used her to remind me about the use of my tongue and how I ought to handle privileged information.

You and I need to make a conscious decision to respond to those inner nudges and whispers of God's Spirit, as He seeks to do the very thing that we could never do: tame our tongue. Whenever the Lord speaks to you and me, and we know it, we need to act on His promptings right away. Why? Because if you say what you know you really shouldn't say, someone is going to be hurt or damaged. Many times, the moment it leaves your lips, you'll experience that sudden, sick feeling that you have seized control of your own life again—and grieved the Spirit of the Lord.

Be Accountable

Be accountable to the Holy Spirit. It's really not very complicated. When He says "Watch it," then watch it. When He says "Don't," then don't. When He says "Hush," then hush. When He says "Bite your tongue," then put your teeth into it. You'll feel that nudge and you'll know deep down, "I really shouldn't be talking about this," or "I shouldn't be saying this," or "This conversation has drifted into something unhealthy." *Listen* to that voice and respond, even if it makes for an awkward moment or two. Even if you come off looking a little silly or overly sensitive. What is that in comparison to pleasing God?

But be accountable to someone else, too. When the day is done and you know you've messed up, tell that friend or prayer partner about it. Say, "You know, I told you I wasn't going to do this anymore, but I just did. I opened my mouth, and what came out wasn't sweetness and light. Would you please pray for me? I don't want to be this way anymore." Every time you admit your sin to that friend and seek his or her prayers, you are growing toward Christlikeness.

Cry Out for Help

Psalm 19:14 says, "Let the words of my mouth and the meditation of my heart be acceptable in Your sight, O LORD, my strength and my redeemer."

Good for you, David! Don't you just love this man's honest, humble prayers in the psalms? *"Lord, You're my strength. You're the One who redeems me. You're the One who can help me do this. I want to please You, but I keep thinking the wrong thoughts and saying the wrong things. Be my help and my strength today!"*

Remember Exodus 19, that beautiful prelude to the tender commandments? This Lord we serve is the same One who swoops down and bears us up on eagles' wings. This is the God who creates a way for us where there is no way and provides for our every need—even in a dead, empty desert. Why would He not give us the strength and ability we need to walk in His commands and obey His Word?

Recommit Your Life to Worship and Praise

The first thing I do when I get on my knees to pray is remind God that I know who He is. "You're my Father," I tell Him. "You're my refuge. You're my redeemer. You're the One who lives within me. You're the author and finisher of my faith. I'm so thankful that You are exactly what and who You have promised to be. I honor Your name. All that You are, You are toward me. I praise You. I thank You for being so good." And then I will go ahead and get into all the stuff I need, and all the things that concern my heart, just like you do. But when I'm just about finished praying, I always go back to the place where I started.

I go back to praise.

Praise is the last thing I want to remember when I get up from my knees and walk away. I want to remember whom I've been conversing with. I've been talking to the One who can do anything, fix anything, change anything. I've given it all to Him, so now I can walk away saying, "God, thank You for letting me be with You for these few moments. I praise You and bless You."

When your mouth is filled with gratitude and thanksgiving, there simply isn't going to be room for false, bitter, or cynical words. When your heart is overflowing with praise, you can climb to the top of a water tower, spread your praise to the winds, and never, never find yourself wishing you could call those words back.

In fact, His praise endures forever.

Lord, it's sobering to think how the father of lies has cast his long shadow over your creation. I look forward to that great Day when all shadows and lies and deception will be banished forever! Forgive me, Lord, for the times I have deceived or spoken untrue, unworthy words. How foolish to

think I could ever hide anything from You! Lord, I want to be a person who builds people up . . .who seeks to strengthen and encourage them. When I am tempted to step toward the shadows and speak ill of someone so that I might look better, bring a holy fear to my heart. Remind me what terrible damage a false word can bring.

And so today, Lord, may people around me feel they're in a "safe place" because I speak only the truth. In the name of the One who is Truth, amen.

"You shall not covet your neighbor's house;
you shall not covet your neighbor's wife,
nor his manservant, nor his maidservant,
nor his ox, nor his donkey,
nor anything that is your neighbor's."

EXODUS 20:17

⟊

TRUE CONTENTMENT

Could you handle a glimpse of Ron Mehl's dark side?

Here's the truth, and it isn't pretty.

I have an unhealthy attraction for briefcases. What can I say? There's something about a trim, elegant briefcase that just catches my eye. There's something about shiny gold snaps that turns my head. Some people study faces while waiting at airport gates. Not me; I study briefcases. And when I see something sleek and new, professional and suave, my mouth starts to water. When I hear the crisp sound of those new gold snaps popping open, I turn and stare in spite of myself.

I'm not much of a shopper, but if I do go to a department store with Joyce, you can usually find me in the briefcase section while she looks around at other stuff. You wouldn't believe some of the high-tech features and materials in today's newer brief-cases.

This past year, I'd been whining around home before Christmas, trying to convince my family to be sensitive to my needs and buy me a certain new briefcase I'd had my eye on. I was sure that if I just had *that* briefcase, my eyes would cease to wander; I would be a contented man at last. So they did it. They bought it for me. The very one I'd longed for. I was elated! But...just the other day I saw one I liked even better. And somehow, that took some of the shine off my new briefcase. I felt a little like a second-class citizen when I walked through the airport.

You see? Where does it stop? Once you start coveting, you're never satisfied. Contentment slips out the back door of your life like an unloved child.

And contentment, I believe, is the bottom line of this final commandment.

God knows very well what happens to people when they are caught up in unbridled envy. What God really intends for us is that we would be contented...contented with who we are... contented with what we have...contented with Him.

A covetous person is someone with a severe craving for the possessions or life circumstances of others. It's not just a casual "wouldn't it be nice if..."; it is strong. *"I want what you have, because I feel that is what will satisfy me and make me happy."*

A covetous individual tends to see the world only in terms of how it benefits his own immediate needs. Short-term satisfaction elbows out long-term goals and deeply held values. After reflecting on this tenth commandment, I've come to a conclusion: I am extremely thankful God doesn't give me everything I ask for. He sees the big picture, while I see only a tiny slice of it. And so much of what I see in that tiny slice of reality is colored with "me."

I remember a time when I was speaking at a conference in some city across the country. I woke up on the morning I was to go home and prayed, "Lord, You know how much I want to get home to Joyce and the boys. As a personal favor to me, please don't let there be any delays or cancellations at the airport."

But when I arrived at the gate, guess what? The lady behind the counter said there were some difficulties, and that the flight would have to be delayed for an hour and twenty-five minutes. I was *so* disappointed. I didn't want to sit for an hour and a half in a crummy airport! Hadn't the Lord heard me that morning? Was I tuned in on the wrong wavelength or something? As I walked away from the counter, I remember thinking, *Why does this always have to happen to me? I love my family so much—I miss them so much. I'll bet nobody in this airport loves their family like I do.*

But what happened next jarred me from that bout of self-pity.

I saw a young man running down the concourse, struggling with his bags, his face white as a sheet. He ran right up to the gate where I was waiting, looked up at the time posted for departure, and said, "Oh, thank God!" And then he told the ticket agent, "I need to get home, and this is the last flight of the day. My little boy was struck by a car. He's in the hospital in serious condition. My wife's alone with him in the hospital."

I sat there and thought, *Lord, I'm so glad You didn't answer my selfish prayer.* I think God used that little incident to help me see how often I'm driven by a desire to meet *my* needs, rather than looking around me a bit and considering that other people might have some needs, too.

The fact is, God knows *exactly* what you and I need. He knows when we need what we need. He knows how much we need of what we need. And He has a way of seeing to it that I receive what I need at just the right time…not my time, perhaps, but the right time.

Can you imagine the hurt of a parent whose child goes to school and tells the administrators and teachers that he doesn't have enough food, a nice enough place to sleep, or decent clothes to wear? The burden of a discontented, ungrateful child would be a heavy weight for any parent to bear. How, then, does our discontentment affect the heart of our heavenly Father? I wonder how much it must pain Him when He sees us eaten up with envy, as if to say, *"What I have isn't good enough. What You have provided is something less than what I deserve."*

Psalm 23 tells us that He is our shepherd, that He will lead us, and that we will have no lack. Hebrews 13:5 (NIV) says, "Keep your lives free from the love of money and be content with what you have, because God has said, 'Never will I leave you; never will I forsake you.'"

Why would the Lord say these things?

Because He knows what coveting and greed will do to a human life. He understands the devastation it will bring, and in His love He would spare us from that.

There is one well-known chain-marketing group that used to begin their pitch with the question, "What are your dreams? Tell me what you'd really like to have for you and your family." And what they want you to do is "dream" in material, self-indulgent terms: a bigger house, a new car, a flashy ski boat, a swimming pool, or a two-week cruise. A friend of mine threw a monkey wrench into that pitch when he replied, "Well, what I really long for doesn't have much to do with money. What I want is a family that loves the Lord and walks with God. What I really want for my children is a heart that is faithful to Christ, no matter what their finances or their circumstances." That reply just wasn't in the script! The canned presentation faltered and stalled. What my friend wanted wasn't something you could cut out of a magazine and tape to your refrigerator.

How many of us have wondered what it would be like to win a lottery or a sweepstakes? Maybe we've even felt a little envious of those huge cash prizes. (Even though we tell ourselves we would surely tithe if God let us win.) I read an article in a newspaper about a couple who won $48.6 million dollars in the lottery several years ago. After winning, the woman said, "We had one month of good times—and three years of misery. I'd trade it all for a normal life. It's not worth it. Health and happiness is what I want."

The woman, Lynette Nichols, is a recovering alcoholic and tranquilizer abuser. She has had three pacemaker operations since her big lottery win. Jimmy Nichols, her husband, writes, "More bad than good came out of this." Jimmy filed for divorce several months after the big win, and legal bills have topped over $200,000 on both sides.

Why would the Lord say, "You shall not covet your neighbor's house; you shall not covet your neighbor's wife, nor his manservant, nor his maidservant, nor his ox, nor donkey, nor anything that is your neighbor's"? Why would He make that the last item of His Ten Commandments? Because God knows a few things about coveting.

He Knows That What We Covet Will Not Last

The very things people long to possess and hold in their hands will eventually slip between their fingers.

Second Corinthians 4:18 (NIV) says:

> So we fix our eyes not on what is seen, but on what is unseen. For what is seen is temporary, but what is unseen is eternal.

The Lord is saying, "Life on earth is uncertain and fragile enough as it is; I want you to concentrate on those things that will last." Clothes aren't going to last. Cars and houses and toys aren't going to last. Those things are temporal. Two seconds after you die, they won't mean a thing to you—they'll be left behind to plague the lives of your children.

Every Christmas we're presented with those "must" items that we simply have to buy for our kids. And every year the Big Thing is something new. One year the gift of choice is a Tickle Me Elmo. People will almost stampede through a store to get one. There have been Pet Rocks, Cabbage Patch Dolls, Chia Pets, and Beanie Babies, to name a few.

But next year it will be something else. Tickle Me Elmo won't be laughing anymore; he'll be languishing on the top shelf of the closet between a SaladShooter and a Vega-Matic. There will always be something new to desire.

Ecclesiastes 5:11 (TLB) says, "The more you have, the more you spend, right up to the limits of your income." Money and material things that aren't properly stewarded will slip through your hands. I just love it when I hear couples say, "The best days of our home and marriage were in the very beginning when we barely had enough to get by. Things were really tight, but we had a lot of laughs. We were never happier."

I've told you about our bedroom in our first apartment. It was so small we only had one little twin-sized mattress for a bed. Joyce was so tiny I would push the mattress up against the wall so I wouldn't kick her out of bed by accident. They're great memories…and we did have a lot of fun. Would I have been happier in a palatial master bedroom in a Select-matic king bed with silk sheets? Not a chance! I wouldn't trade those memories for anything.

He Knows That What We Covet Will Be a Burden to Us

If you don't believe that, read Psalm 51. David had coveted his neighbor's wife. And because he was in a position to take whatever he wanted, he took her. Psalm 51 was written in the aftermath. They are the words of a broken man…a man who longed with all his heart to turn back the clock but knew he could not. He wrote:

> I admit my shameful deed—it haunts me day and night.
> It is against you and you alone I sinned and did this terrible thing. You saw it all…. (Psalm 51:3–4, TLB)

For the rest of his days David endured the wrenching emotions of a man who watched his family sink into heartbreak and ruin. Rape, murder, incest, disgrace, betrayal, rebellion…it never stopped.

David had thought, "There's an empty place inside me, and

if I could just possess Uriah's wife, I think I would be satisfied and fulfilled." But David discovered something worse than an empty place in his heart. It was a heart shattered into ten thousand pieces.

God knows how burdensome the things we covet can become in our lives. The weight of them can distract us, press down on us, and squeeze all of the simple joys out of life.

He Knows That Covetousness Is Destructive

No one said it more clearly than Paul to his young friend, Timothy:

> But godliness with contentment is great gain. For we brought nothing into the world, and we can take nothing out of it. But if we have food and clothing, we will be content with that. *People who want to get rich fall into temptation and a trap and into many foolish and harmful desires that plunge men into ruin and destruction. For the love of money is a root of all kinds of evil. Some people, eager for money, have wandered from the faith and pierced themselves with many griefs.* (1 Timothy 6:6–10, NIV)

Paul tells Timothy that people who long to be rich soon begin to do all kinds of wrong things to get more money…things that bring them and their families great hurt. They work and scheme and squeeze themselves dry to get what they think will bring them happiness. But in the end, they don't have any time or energy for the people who are truly important…the people they love the most.

That is why some counselors say the number one cause of

divorce today is finances. Money unwisely spent becomes a breeding ground for arguments and fights. Covetousness brings about destruction, divorce, and death.

He Knows That Covetousness Is Deceptive

In Luke 12:15 (NIV), Jesus says: "Watch out! Be on your guard against all kinds of greed; a man's life does not consist in the abundance of his possessions."

Do we truly believe that? Do we believe that down deep in our bones, so that the truth of those words changes our priorities, impacts our choices, and shapes the way we live our lives? We live in a consumer society, and today's sophisticated marketers spend billions of dollars and work around the clock for one purpose: to make you unhappy and dissatisfied with what you have. With all of their considerable skill, talent, and training, they seek to convince you and I that if we would just buy *this* or possess *that*, we'd find a greater measure of happiness and security in this old world.

Is "new" really better? I think my favorite car of all was our family's old Chevy station wagon. The Brown Beauty. We went everywhere in that wagon. I can still remember all nine of us running from the house to the car in a mad dash to claim the front seat. Failing that, we'd grab the door handle and holler, "Window! Window! I get the window!" We'd joke and laugh and fight in the backseats. Like kids everywhere since the beginning of time, we'd yell, "You're in my seat!" or "You're on *my part* of the seat!" Mom would reach back and draw lines so that we wouldn't invade one another's territories.

Our Chevy wagon was the best. We played games and even

ate our sack lunches in that car. My friends would always brag about their families' new, big, expensive cars. But their cars weren't as much fun because, before you got in, you had to clean off your shoes. And you couldn't eat candy or ice cream in *their* cars.

When we traveled to Grandma's house, my stepdad would put boards in the back of our wagon so more of us could lie down and sleep, since it was a long trip and we never stopped at a motel. Now, what am I saying? That everyone should drive an old station wagon with rust spots in the paint and gum wads under the seats? No, I'm simply making this point: if you believe it takes newer, nicer, more luxurious things to make you happy, you are deceived.

Our value does not lie in what we possess.

Is that a revolutionary thought?

Our value doesn't spring from what we wear, what we drive, or where we live. Our value is wrapped up in the amazing fact that Jesus Christ, the mighty Son of God and Creator of the world, loved us enough to die for us. He is the One who gives worth and value to our lives. He paid the price and purchased our salvation. But when it comes to those material things of our lives, there will always be something better, something nicer, something newer (or in the case of computers, something *faster*). Coveting such things is a dead-end street, and it is extremely deceptive.

I've known pastors who continually covet a larger ministry. Once they pass the 500-member barrier in their church, they're not happy until it's 1000. Is that the top of the heap? No, it isn't. Before long you read about a guy who graduated with you from

Bible college who has 5,000 members in his church. But if you can get 5,000, you ought to be able to get 10,000—and a national television ministry to boot.

Paul wrote, "But they, measuring themselves by themselves, and comparing themselves among themselves, are not wise" (2 Corinthians 10:12).

What great words of counsel. Don't play the comparison game. Don't compare yourself with others. Don't toy with those thoughts in the back of your mind. Don't look at the guy in the next office or the couple in the house next door. Don't measure yourself by the things others have. Don't compare yourself with what someone else has accomplished or attained. Don't go around with a measuring tape seeing how much they have or how far they've gone compared to how much you have and how far you've gone. If you have more, it'll just make you proud. If you have less, you'll become envious and begin to covet.

People say, "When I get that car, then I'll really be happy." Or "When I find that right person and get married, then I'll finally be happy." Or "When we finally get some children, we'll get along better and we'll be happy." Or "When we finally get that vacation home in the mountains, we'll all do things together as a family, and we'll be happy."

Can your family have just as much fun in a tent as in a Winnebago?

Could life be just as full bouncing along in an old Jeep as in a forty-thousand-dollar Ford Expedition?

Can a husband and wife who delight in one another enjoy a dinner of hot dogs and beans by candlelight as much as stuffed pheasant with plum sauce under glass in some five-star restaurant?

Can you tell time with a ten-dollar Timex as well as you can with a thousand-dollar Rolex?

Discontentment really has very little to do with "what you have." If you are unhappy as a single person and believe that marriage is going to make you happy, you are deceived. If you are not satisfied, happy, and fulfilled in who you are, where you are, and what you have, changing your circumstances will not be an instant ticket to joy. Oh, how disappointed and dissatisfied we can become when we realize that the things we finally possess after long waiting are *not* the things that bring satisfaction or lasting contentment to our lives.

He Knows That Contentment Is a Process

Scripture is very clear about that. In Philippians 4:11 (NIV), Paul writes: "I have learned to be content whatever the circumstances." He *learned* contentment from the Lord. It didn't happen overnight. J. B. Phillips paraphrased Paul's words like this:

> I know now how to live when things are difficult and I know how to live when things are prosperous. In general and in particular I have learned the secret of facing either plenty or poverty. I am ready for anything through the strength of the one who lives within me. (Philippians 4:12–13, Phillips)

Do I have to have that accomplishment, or that set of circumstances, or those particular possessions to make me happy?

Every experience that you and I face is an opportunity to learn and practice contentment in our Lord.

We've already quoted Hebrews 13:5: *Be content with what you have.* Why? Because He will never leave us or forsake us. God will never leave me, the Holy Spirit will never leave me, Jesus Christ will never leave me. My times of need become opportunities for God to show me again and again how He—in Himself and in fellowship with Him—will fill all those empty places in my heart.

Paul reminds Timothy that we didn't bring anything into this world, and we won't take anything out. (1 Timothy 6:7). Absolutely nothing. We didn't come into this world with a penny in our hand, and we won't go out with one. Someone may stuff a penny into your hand after you've passed away, but you won't be taking it anywhere!

Attitude is everything, because if we don't learn to be content with our present situation, then we'll face the same circumstances again and again. That's why the children of Israel wandered in circles for forty years in the Sinai wilderness. Around and around they went, year after weary year, seeing the same scrawny trees, the same boring rocks, the same shriveled-up bushes. They experienced the same thing over and over again. That's why you hear yourself say, "Well, here we go again. Déjà vu! We've gone through this a million times."

And you *are* going to go through it. Again and again. Until what? Until you realize that contentment is something learned. When Paul says, "I've learned..." do you know what he means? He is saying, "I remember the days when I wasn't very content. I had to learn contentment. I wasn't always patient and content, but I *learned.*" There must have been times when Paul felt impatient and thought, "God, why don't You do this, or provide this, or give me this?" But Paul finally learned where to find what he'd always been looking for. And when he did, everything else paled in comparison.

> I once thought all these things were so very important, but now I consider them worthless because of what Christ has done. Yes, everything else is worthless when compared with the priceless gain of knowing Christ Jesus my Lord. I have discarded everything else, counting it all as garbage. (Philippians 3:7–8, NLT)

Once Paul found the true, artesian source of contentment, everything else tasted like flat Coke.

God Knows That True Contentment Brings Peace

People lust after possessions and success and all those things yet pay a tremendous price for it in their family and their home. They want more and more but are never satisfied.

Is it wrong to want success in your life? Is that a problem, you ask? No, I hope you are as successful as you can be. But if that's the aim and goal of your life, I will tell you that when you get there (wherever "there" may be), it won't be enough.

I have a friend, Ron Rearick, who, before he became a Christian, extorted a million dollars from United Airlines. He picked up the money at the designated drop site and sat in his car counting the bundles in the briefcase. It was all there. One million dollars in the front seat with him. But the only thought that kept going through his mind that day was, *This isn't enough. I should have asked for more.*

When I say that contentment brings peace, what do I mean? I mean that it is in those personal times with God—even in the midst of difficult, heartbreaking circumstances—that you and I learn true contentment. The psalmist wrote:

> Nevertheless I am continually with You;
>> you hold me by my right hand.
> You will guide me with Your counsel,
>> and afterward receive me to glory.
> Whom have I in heaven but You?
> And there is none upon earth that I desire besides You.
> My flesh and my heart fail;
>> but God is the strength of my heart
>> and my portion forever.
> (Psalm 73:23–26)

Do you know why I feel contentment in those moments I spend in His presence? Because I know God is going to take care of everything. He's going to work everything out. He's going to arrange it all. I *know* that.

God knows what happened a millennium ago. If you asked Him what happened a thousand years ago, He could describe every detail of every minute of the day in every corner of this world. And He could tell you also what's going to happen a thousand years from now, when everything you've ever owned will have dissolved into fine dust. So I guess He might be able to figure out the remainder of this life for you and me!

Why shouldn't I covet my neighbor's house or wife or the things that he has? Because God knows that once we begin to walk down that road, we will never, never get enough. No matter how much it is, it won't be sufficient.

David Robinson, superstar center for the San Antonio Spurs, spoke about watching Michael Jordan embrace the Chicago Bulls' first championship trophy "as if a piece of metal could validate a life."

"Here I am," said the star athlete, "with five cars, two houses and more money than I ever thought I'd have. What more could I ask for? But where am I going? Here's Michael Jordan. He has more than me and boy, I'd like to have some of the things he has. But is the world setting a trap for us?

"What I had should have been plenty," he adds. "But no matter how much I had, it didn't seem like enough because material things can't satisfy your deepest needs. That's when I started to realize that I needed the Lord."[1]

Whatever your circumstance today—this very moment— He can make your cup overflow.

Even if you drive an old brown station wagon.

And yes, even if you carry last year's briefcase. You see, I'm learning, too.

Lord, You said I shouldn't covet. But sometimes in my weakness I've reached out for things that I thought would satisfy me. Yet once I possessed them, Lord, they seemed like cheap counterfeits. They didn't satisfy me at all. Lord,

I wish I were more careful to listen to You! Then I wouldn't have to learn everything the hard way. You've clearly said You were committed to supplying my every need. Please, gracious Lord, help me to surrender my selfish desires. Help me to learn the true contentment that comes from You alone.

And so today, Lord, I will covet only those things that You know will satisfy me and fulfill me. In Jesus' name, amen.

CONCLUSION

My wife's all-time favorite movie is *Fiddler on the Roof.* I'll bet she's watched it at least twenty-five times. I had only seen bits and pieces of it until she recently persuaded me to actually sit down with her for a few hours and watch the whole thing, beginning to end.

Now, when *I* watch a movie at home, I like to sit back, be quiet, concentrate on the movie, and maybe crunch on a little popcorn. Not Joyce. It seemed like every five seconds she was hitting me on the shoulder or squeezing my knee and saying, "Here it comes. Get ready. Watch this. You're going to love this."

Because she has seen it so many times, she knows every song, every word of dialogue. And after twenty-five viewings (this amazes me), she still cries in all the sad or tender places. I think she wanted me to cry, too, but I'm tough as tempered steel (yeah, right).

For me, this is a picture of how well God knows us. He sees everything. Nothing is hidden from Him. Just as Joyce knows every person, every line, every expression, every scene change, and every note of every song in that movie, so our God sees and knows every detail of our lives—even before it happens. Every joy and every sigh. Every hardship and every song. He knows them all. God knows everything about us, and as Proverbs 2:8

(NIV) tells us, "He guards the course of the just and protects the way of his faithful ones."

How does He guard your path in life? Many ways. And one of those ways is through His Ten Commandments. Oh, how they reveal His heart! All the way through the Scriptures, you see it...the Lord's care for us. He always seems to be there.

The psalmist said in Psalm 119:97, "Oh, how I love Your law! It is my meditation all the day."

He was saying, "Lord, I just love Your Word. Your law means everything to me. I think about it over and over again as the days of my life speed by."

In an earlier chapter we said that God's Word is like a fence that keeps us separated from danger. That may be so, but do people meditate about fences? Do we sit back and reflect on boards and white pickets and barbed wire in our quiet moments? Probably not. But we *would* meditate on a love letter from the dearest person in our lives, wouldn't we? And that's what I've been trying to demonstrate in the reflections I've gathered in this book. The Ten Commandments are, more than anything else, a full-hearted love letter from God to His people. A fence? Yes, that too. But listen for a moment to the excitement—the *passion*—in the psalmist's voice as he describes his experience with the commands of God's Word:

> I meditate on your precepts and consider your ways.
> I delight in your decrees; I will not neglect your word....
> My soul is consumed with longing for your laws at all
>   times....

Your statutes are my delight; they are my counselors....

I run in the path of your commands, for you have set my
    heart free....

Direct me in the path of your commands, for there I find
    delight....

The law from your mouth is more precious to me than
    thousands of pieces of silver and gold.

(Psalm 119:15–16, 20, 24, 32, 35, 72, NIV)

Why should I love His commands? Why should I love those things with all of my heart?

Because His Word Will Keep Me from Disaster

My friend Larry told me about one of the first bike rides (sans training wheels) he attempted with his young son Matthew. Going down a hill near their home on the east side of Portland, little Matt lost control of his bike. When the bike crashed, Matt went over the handlebars, landed on his head, and scooted along the asphalt for several feet...on the top of his helmet.

When Matthew got up off the ground okay, just a little shaken, Larry looked at the helmet and saw that its top—and not the top of his little son's head!—had been badly scraped and scored by the rough asphalt. How do you think Larry felt about that helmet? He loved that helmet. He kissed that helmet. He valued and honored that helmet, and used it as an object lesson for his boy.

Proverbs 13:13 says:

He who despises the word will be destroyed,
>   but he who fears the commandment will be rewarded."

A person who resists, scorns, and rejects God's Word will meet with destruction. I wish I could say it in a nicer way, but I know it to be true and no overstatement. As a pastor I see it all the time. It's one of those things that turns a pastor's hair prematurely gray. People say, "I don't need God, and I don't need His Word. I don't care about His commands and requirements. I don't care to hear His warnings. I'll do what I want to do." That person's life will come to disaster in one way or another—and God's Word is not shy about saying so.

Because His Word Brings Deep Satisfaction

When you're hiking in the wilderness, you're foolish if you don't bring along a map and a compass. Those items are as basic to survival as a canteen and a box of waterproof matches. In the same way, without the direction and counsel of God's Word, you will end up wandering around in circles. In fact, you will waste your life.

Psalm 119:92–93 (TLB), says: "I would have despaired and perished unless Your laws had been my deepest delight. I will never lay aside your laws, for you have used them to restore my joy and health."

There are people who say, "Well, *I* don't respond to God's love and His commands, and look how well off I am. Look at how much I have. Look at how much I've achieved." I'm not suggesting that these people couldn't have achieved financial success apart from the Word, *but they will never be satisfied.* In the end they will say, "I've accumulated all this, done all this, accomplished all this, and worked very, very hard…but I've never really found a purpose for living. I've never found out why I'm here on this planet, or what God wanted me to do with my life." That's a pretty empty, desolate thing to realize as your approach the end of your days.

Because His Word Provides a Foundation for My Life

In a small Kansas town a number of years ago, many of the residents were gathered in the high school gymnasium for a basketball game. Things were going well for the home team, and the partisans had reason to stomp, clap, and cheer. But what happened at halftime changed that little town forever.

The fans packed into the gym were suddenly rocked by a powerful explosion—the kind you feel deep in your chest—and everyone ran outside to see what had happened. As it turned out, the town's massive grain elevator had collapsed and fallen across a small nursery school. Five little children died that day.

What could have caused such a disaster? What could have brought about such a shocking event? After a close inspection of the grain elevator's foundation, investigators discovered that termites had eaten the heart out of the beams and rafters, leaving only a deceptive, empty shell. What subtle devastation these insects can work on a structure! The damage is difficult to discern because their insidious activity is hidden from the eye.

I often wonder if that isn't what happens to the lives of those who disregard God's loving word to them. I wonder if our indifference to God's commands doesn't allow the spiritual termites to eat away at our life and character, which ends up bringing us down. Maybe that's why when someone falls morally, you hear people say, "How could this happen? How could this be? Everything looked fine. We never saw this coming."

God's original intention was that His Word would be the foundation of my life, to stabilize me through life's many storms. Obedience to these commands of God isn't like insanity, where you continually do the same thing and never get any results. Faithful obedience to God is the very pathway to the richest life you can possibly live. Psalm 19 reaffirms this over and over again. If you're looking for a piece of Scripture to commit to memory, place this psalm on your short list of candidates!

In verse 7, the text says God's Word will make you wise.

> The testimony of the LORD is sure,
>   making wise the simple.

The word *simple* means undiscerning. It means I really can't distinguish between good and bad, right and wrong. How appropriate this concern is for today, as all the lines of morality and righteousness are being deliberately warped and blurred. The Lord's commands will help you when you find yourself saying, "Should I or shouldn't I? Is this right or wrong? Is this a good idea or a bad one? Will this help me or destroy me? I really don't know." The Lord says, "If you will walk in obedience to My commands, you will became an extremely wise person, where you once were naive or undiscerning."

The other day a friend of mine was commenting about some of her relatives. She spoke about how one particular family seemed to lurch from one ill-advised, disastrous decision to another. They would get into one scrape and then do something impulsive to change the situation only to land in a far worse situation. It seemed to my friend that this family's whole life was a picture of bouncing from one bad, foolish choice to another…from one calamity to the next. They were undiscerning. It was as though they were thrashing about in the dark, or trying to drive somewhere with no map, no compass, no road signs, and no clear idea where they were headed.

Our loving Father never intended life to be led in such a way. That's why He provided us with His tender commandments.

Verse 8 (NIV) of Psalms 19 says that God's commands will bring joy to your heart and life.

> The precepts of the LORD are right,
> > giving joy to the heart.

You and I hear people say, "I'm not happy," or "I just want to be happy." So people will counsel, "Go on a cruise. Buy a car. Use your credit cards and have a good time." But the psalmist says, "What brings joy to my heart, Lord, are Your Word and promises."

Do you know why? Because now I don't ever have to worry about another thing. I know now, Lord, that when I trust in You, obey Your Word, and follow You, You make Yourself responsible for me. You're responsible for dealing with my past, showing me where to go today, and directing me into a productive future. "My life is in Your hands." What release and joy those thoughts bring! It is so wearing and so tiring to try to be a "fixer" in life, continually trying to manipulate things and people to achieve desired outcomes. The scheming and the worrying become exhausting…and really aren't effective, anyway. How much better to focus my energies on Him and trust Him to deal with the details of my life.

Joy to the heart? This description of the Lord's commands runs directly counter to Satan's arguments. Isn't the Lord a killjoy? Aren't people who follow God's commands grim, colorless, and uptight, with no sense of fun, no sense of humor? Isn't that how Hollywood and the entertainment industry have portrayed Christians for generations?

We shouldn't be surprised; it's just one more element of Satan's ongoing smear campaign.

Verse 8 (NIV) also says God's commands will enlighten your eyes.

> The commands of the LORD are radiant,
>> giving light to the eyes.

Do you know what that means? It means the Lord turns the light on. Maybe as a young man or young woman thinking about getting married, you have had a parent say to you, "Be careful who you marry. This is for a lifetime! You want to make very sure you scrutinize everything about this person." But it's so difficult being detached and objective when you're in love!

Listen, *the Bible will turn the light on for you!* If you can't see, are confused, and aren't sure what you're looking at or what you've got, the Lord says to you, "I'll turn the lights on. I'll enlighten your eyes. I'll help you to see more keenly than you ever thought you could see."

Verse 9 says that this Word is going to endure forever, so you can always turn to it.

> The fear of the LORD is pure, enduring forever.
> The ordinances of the LORD are sure and altogether righteous.

It's eternal. It will always be there. It will never be adjusted, mothballed, downsized, or discredited. And it is altogether righteous, which simply means it is right through and through.

Some people outside of Christ think we're insane for putting our trust in the Bible and depending on the Lord Jesus the way we do. They say we're "emotional cripples" for having to lean on something outside ourselves. And to those comments I reply... *"Amen."* Absolutely. You want me to wear those labels? Hand 'em over and I'll put 'em on. I'm not ashamed to say there are days when I have *no idea* how I'm going to make it through. I am sustained and helped when I lean on the cross, when I lean on His Word. If leaning hard on God makes me handicapped in the eyes of the world, then bring on the wheelchair. I'm not ashamed to admit my TOTAL dependence upon Him.

Eagles' Wings

"I bore them on eagles' wings," the Lord reminded Moses.

He still does. He's still doing that today. He's still swooping down and helping. He's still plucking us out of free fall and soaring into the heavens while we hang on for the ride. Do you know why? Because we can't live by these commands in our own strength. We can't fulfill them. We can't do it. As many have correctly said, the Christian life isn't difficult, it's *impossible*. Only He can enable me to live this way, and I am deceived to think otherwise.

Jesus said, "Do not think that I came to destroy the Law or the Prophets. I did not come to destroy but to fulfill" (Matthew 5:17). How true. He is the One who fulfills all things for me. Hallelujah! God's own Son came down from heaven so that I could trust in Him and depend on Him to help me do what I could never do.

When I was in Bible college, I had to memorize Romans 8. Frankly, I hated that assignment. It seemed like busywork. Why in the world would I ever have to know those verses? Looking back now, I realize that, along with meeting Joyce, that was one of the best things that happened to me in college. I'm so glad we had that assignment. I'm so glad I learned Romans 8 early on in my ministry. I've depended upon it ever since. Verses 3–4 say,

> For what the law could not do in that it was weak through the flesh, God did by sending His own Son in the likeness of sinful flesh, on account of sin: He condemned sin in the flesh, that the righteous requirement of the law might be fulfilled in us who do not walk according to the flesh but according to the Spirit.

In other words, Jesus came down to make it possible for me to live this way. Only He could fulfill those things in my heart and life. I couldn't do this! But He could...and can. I can't fulfill the law. But He can. Paul tells us, "I have been crucified with Christ. I myself no longer live, but Christ lives in me. So I live my life in this earthly body by trusting in the Son of God, who loved me and gave himself for me." (Galatians 2:19–20, NLT).

I'm reminded of the story of a very wealthy man who, along with his son, shared a passion for collecting art. Together they traveled around the world, adding only the finest treasures to their collection. Priceless works by Picasso, Van Gogh, Monet, and many others adorned the walls of the family estate. The widowed elder man looked on with satisfaction as his only child became an experienced art collector in his own right. The son's trained eye and sharp business mind caused his father to beam with pride as they dealt with art dealers around the world.

As winter approached one year, war engulfed the nation, and the young man left to serve his country. After only a few short weeks, his father received a telegram. His beloved son was missing in action. The art collector awaited more news, fearing he would never see his son again. Within days, his worst fears were confirmed. The young man had died while attempting to evacuate a wounded fellow soldier.

Distraught and lonely, the old man faced the upcoming Christmas holidays with dread. What was left to celebrate? His joy was gone.

Early on Christmas morning, a knock on the door awakened the grieving man. As he walked to the door, the masterpieces of art on the walls seemed to mock him. Of what value were they without his son to share in their beauty? Opening the someone exclaimed, "Now we can get on with it."

But at that moment, the auctioneer looked up at the audience and quietly announced that the auction was over. Stunned disbelief blanketed the room. Finally someone spoke up. "What do you mean, it's over? We didn't come here for a picture of some old guy's son. What about all of these paintings? There are millions of dollars' worth of art here! I demand that you explain what is going on!"

The auctioneer replied, "It's very simple. According to the will of the father, whoever takes the son...gets it all."

And so it is with you and me.

Why am I able to please God and walk in His commands? *Because of the Son.*

Why do I enjoy forgiveness of sins and companionship with the Father? *Because of the Son.*

Why do I have eternal life? *Because of the Son.*

Why do I enjoy such rich treasures of friendship, family, and a task in life that demands my best and promises eternal awards? *Because of the Son.* Only because of God's Son.

I don't deserve a bit of it. I don't deserve a second glance from God, yet He has made me His adopted child and a coheir of the universe with the Lord Jesus Christ Himself. It doesn't make any sense to me. Why should someone like me receive the treasures of heaven? All I did was take His Son to be my Savior. Yet God, in His incomprehensible love and wisdom, whispers something in my ear.

"When you take My Son, you get it all."

‿❦‿

Chapter 7
Removing the Seeds of Murder

1. World Magazine, December 13, 1997.

Chapter 8
God's Fence Around Your Marriage

1. C. S. Lewis, *The Magician's Nephew* (New York, N.Y.: Harper Collins Publishers, Inc., 1955), 44.

Chapter 11
True Contentment

1. David Hubbard, *Faith in Sports: Athletes and Their Religion On and Off the Field* (New York, N.Y.: Doubleday and Company, Inc., 1998).